I0361491

Avoidant Attachment

Journey to Secure Attachment through Effective Relationship

(How to Avoid Being Awkward and Have Better Conversations in Business)

Harvey Daniels

Published By **Frank Joseph**

Harvey Daniels

All Rights Reserved

Avoidant Attachment: Journey to Secure Attachment through Effective Relationship (How to Avoid Being Awkward and Have Better Conversations in Business)

ISBN 978-1-7772636-8-3

No part of this guidebook shall be reproduced in any form without permission in writing from the publisher except in the case of brief quotations embodied in critical articles or reviews.

Legal & Disclaimer

The information contained in this book is not designed to replace or take the place of any form of medicine or professional medical advice. The information in this book has been provided for educational & entertainment purposes only.

The information contained in this book has been compiled from sources deemed reliable, and it is accurate to the best of the Author's knowledge; however, the Author cannot guarantee its accuracy and validity and cannot be held liable for any errors or omissions. Changes are periodically made to this book. You must consult your doctor or get professional medical advice before using any of the suggested remedies, techniques, or information in this book.

Upon using the information contained in this book, you agree to hold harmless the Author from and against any damages, costs, and expenses, including any legal fees potentially resulting from the application of any of the information provided by this guide. This disclaimer applies to any damages or injury caused by the use and application, whether directly or indirectly, of any advice or information presented, whether for breach of contract, tort, negligence, personal injury, criminal intent, or under any other cause of action.

You agree to accept all risks of using the information presented inside this book. You need to consult a professional medical practitioner in order to ensure you are both able and healthy enough to participate in this program.

Table Of Contents

Chapter 1: Avoidant Attachment in Relationship 1

Chapter 2: How to Show Up For Your Avoidant Partner 15

Chapter 3: How To Overcome Avoidant Attachment 22

Chapter 4: How to Increase Communication.......................................37

Chapter 5: The Anxious-Avoidant Dance 50

Chapter 6: Ending The Anxious-Avoidant Dance 67

Chapter 7: Avoidant Attachment Key Characteristics.......................................83

Chapter 8: Defining Avoidant Attachment 94

Chapter 9: Key Indicators of Avoidant Attachment 108

Chapter 10: Exercises for Attachment Reflection 117

Chapter 11: Crafting Your Personal Growth Action Plan 141

Chapter 12: Inspiring Success Stories.... 150

Chapter 13: Understanding Avoidant Attachment 155

Chapter 14: Rewriting Limiting Beliefs .. 164

Chapter 15: Building Secure Relationships 173

Chapter 16: Healing Inner Child Wounds 177

Chapter 1: Avoidant Attachment in Relationship

It can be tough to cope with an avoidant attachment fashion in a dating.

Adults with an avoidant attachment fashion are usually self-directed, impartial, and uncomfortable with emotional intimacy and closeness. In today's, they appear like self-confident, confident, and on pinnacle of factors of their lives.

Avoidant attaches are often extraordinarily a fulfillment because of the fact they recognition their energy on their careers in place in their relationships.

Someone with an avoidant attachment fashion may additionally have many buddies or friends because of the reality they may be an entire lot of a laugh to be spherical. Despite the truth that they are no longer lonely, their connections are commonly superficial, and that they never want emotional guide from others.

Being in a relationship with an avoidant companion is difficult because of the truth, on the equal time as an avoidant attacher will engage in relationships, they do not virtually allow the opportunity character "in." Instead, they erect non-public partitions or obstacles to keep away from closeness and emotional intimacy with others, which prevents the development of fine and deep connections.

Furthermore, as quickly as a romantic courting starts to turn into a greater significant connection, an avoidant accomplice usually closes off and withdraws from the other individual. Such human beings might also even search for insignificant reasons to end a dating, like a accomplice's inconsequential actions, appearance, or slightly traumatic conduct.

How an avoidant attachment fashion increase

Most humans who've avoidant attachment in maturity had caregivers who failed to famend or meet their desires after they have been little.

Commonly, the parents of these human beings had them younger. However, now and again the mother and father have been certainly experiencing their non-public highbrow misery in the route in their kids. For example, probable their private mother and father died, or possibly their partner (your different decide) deserted them. The pain of every of those conditions also can motive the determine to be more concerned with their very private healing than with their infant. Oof.

Children who growth up in volatile environments also can increase this attachment fashion. Being accompanied, switching foster houses, looking their parents' divorce, or experiencing the dearth of existence of 1 or each in their mother and father all offer the first-class surroundings for growing this attachment fashion.

Children in those environments in no way had someone on whom they'll depend for normal smooth loving care.

As a prevent cease result, they needed to discover ways to stay on with out that validation, love, or help from an external supply. In many times, those youngsters should learn how to deny the significance of their emotions. As a stop end result, even as those people attain adulthood, they haven't any idea a way to acquire such care from a person else.

To be smooth, avoidant attachment is not just like being aromantic. People in every elegance may be tired of romance.

However, one (having an avoidant attachment fashion) is normally rooted in adolescence trauma that, if addressed, could probable appreciably beautify the pleasant of one's life. And the possibility (being aromantic) is a very ordinary and healthy identity that doesn't necessitate the intervention of a highbrow health expert.

Signs of avoidant attachment style

Simply positioned, humans with avoidant attachment patterns avoid, avoid, and avoid a few more.

They keep away from stepping into relationships, emotional closeness, and counting on others. So, if you need to apprehend if someone has avoidant attachment, ask your self whether or not or no longer that character leans into or flees from closeness.

When you try to investigate greater approximately their internal emotional international, what verbal response do you get? They also can have an avoidant attachment fashion in the event that they emerge as agitated, brush aside the importance of the communique, or accuse you of being needy or clingy.

Take word in their body language at some stage in those encounters as properly. These human beings usually bodily withdraw at the first sign of intimacy and end up rather awkward. During such an exchange, a person with avoidant attachment may moreover try to located bodily distance amongst you, which includes at the sofa. Alternatively, they may start chewing on their sleeve, biting their nail, keeping off their gaze, bouncing their knee, or acting out some thing their non-public tension-inform is.

If you recall this man or woman to be one of the most self-enough humans , they may moreover have avoidant attachment. True, independence is commonly regarded as a fantastic (nay, amazing!) individual trait. However, because maximum human beings with avoidant attachment styles did not have someone on whom they'll depend as kids, they frequently become exceptionally independent—normally as a way to live on.

These people now not often placed themselves in conditions in which they need to rely upon others. That may be visible in their refusal to permit someone else do the laundry or grocery buying, or in their incapacity to invite for words of encouragement or a hug on a hard or disturbing day.

Avoidant attachers can be in particular tough to break due to their tendency to maintain their internal worlds personal and avoid emotionally tough conversations. People who are avoidantly linked are vulnerable to shutting down, numbing, inflexible compartmentalization, and pushing away. And these suppression strategies should make their companions experience "exactly like rejection," making it hard to method—and therefore understand—avoidants!

The bloodless, far off, walled-up avoidant prototype is one I am all too familiar with—because of the fact I, too, am avoidantly related. And strolling thru how that manifested in my youngsters and manifests in my romantic relationships has been the principle consciousness of my treatment artwork over the last years. I grew up with parents who have been often dismissive or punishing of my emotions, which taught me that vulnerability is volatile and that I need to maintain my feelings to myself. That meant growing the belief that exceptional human beings need to now not be relied on to meet my desires in huge. I advanced into someone who values independence and self-control—and who struggles to attain out for assist once I need it. "I can deal with it myself," became my mantra.

As an person, I every so often experience and act determined to avoid emotionality in myself and others. Vulnerability is tough for me (certainly hard—it from time to time reasons a visceral feeling of disgust). It can take a long term for me to absolutely receive as proper with and allow down my defenses. I want extra by myself time and area to approach and modify my emotions than specific humans. When there may be a conflict, I close down psychologically and emerge as shielding, every so often even degrading others for expressing their emotions. I'm moreover liable to misinterpreting feedback as grievance.

If this describes you, you aren't by myself: According to Hazan and Shaver's seminal art work from the Eighties, in which they analyzed 620 self-suggested questionnaires, avoidant attachers account for 25% of the population—a determine that Dr. Levine believes may be even better now.

Those those who're avoidantly related are regularly misunderstood as stoic or as having our shit collectively, whilst in reality, we've got got were given deep relational fears (generally of becoming enmeshed with our partners and dropping our independence) and are in want of care. However, our disability to revel in steady enough to percent our emotional worlds leaves our companions careworn and uncertain a way to take care of us.

To be clean, getting beyond this want to preferably be regularly our duty. Those people who are avoidantly related endure as a good buy obligation as all people else in know-how our relational styles—in all in their glory and damage—and working closer to getting to know new abilties to show up greater effectively.

People who are avoidantly related may additionally additionally battle with interest of approaches we are showing up (and why it's miles risky), however it's far a myth that avoidants are tons much less probably to artwork on recuperation their attachment than the ones who've one of a kind attachment patterns. Working with a therapist is, of route, a remarkable way to apprehend your trauma and accurate related behaviors. Also, do no longer underestimate the importance of safe relationships. Healing relationships can help humans song their attachment structures to a feel of safety. Any prolonged-term, emotionally intimate connection, along with friendship, may be an incredible region to workout noticing and requesting what you need from someone.

If you want to be in a relationship with someone who's avoidantly related, particularly if you select out as anxiously related, you may need to art work on yourself as well as the manner to make your avoidant associate revel in extra secure.

Don't get me incorrect: There's a distinction between a person who acts like a jerk (say, stringing you along aspect sporadic communication) and a person who has avoidant attachment tendencies however is also a being worried and supportive partner. If each unique person's avoidant behaviors make you apprehensive or boom different pink flags, this is a fantastically suitable reason to stop a courting—no matter how plenty work the avoidant character is installing! You have to in no manner be compelled to stay in relationships that do not enjoy real to you, and attachment differences may be in particular difficult.

But if you're searching out strategies to decorate your courting collectively together with your avoidant partner, I actually have right information: it's far possible. The first-class manner to paintings with, in area of within the direction of, your companion's attachment is to normally have a tendency to their internal attachment device in advance than it becomes activated.

So, whether or now not you are avoidantly connected or care about a person who's (or each), permit me to be the avoidant whisperer and provide an cause of what takes region psychologically in relationships for masses people, in addition to how our companions can help us.

Chapter 2: How to Show Up For Your Avoidant Partner

Here is what to understand about how avoidant show up—and ways to expose up for us.

Avoidant attachers, like something else associated with human feelings and behavior, are not the entire equal. The specifics of the manner avoidant attachment manifests—and the manner to navigate a courting with an avoidant attacher—can vary from character to man or woman. However, there are some massive strokes that experts at the problem and avoidant attachers themselves locate useful to apprehend.

Our caregivers' misattunement harmed us notably. Parenting that is cold, remote, crucial, or overly centered on fulfillment or appearance can create an surroundings wherein the child learns that they may be better off relying on themselves. Our brains were conditioned as children to understand vulnerability as inclined factor—on a survival degree. Everything that accompanied in existence changed into constructed on pinnacle of this foundation. We are not on the lookout for to be difficult in our independence. Our brains are in reality now not programmed to perform a little factor else.

We truely crave intimacy. Avoidants revel in intense feelings which consist of deep and eating love. We truly want to revel in stable in our independence before we will open up and be part of. In his exercising with customers and in his upcoming e-book, Dr. Levine draws a parallel among gaining the take shipping of as true with of avoidant attachers and winning over outdoor cats: "Leave the meals out and they may come," he says. In one in all a type phrases, deliver us time and location to assemble accept as proper with in something way works high-quality for you, and we will ultimately enjoy steady with you.

We experience loads. Adults who are avoidantly connected are feeling hundreds greater than we're letting on. When we're emotionally distressed, we have a propensity to show inward rather than outward. If we're shutting down, it's miles in all likelihood because of the fact we're feeling beaten thru emotion. "Big feelings can be overwhelming and tough to specific," Iris says. “As a quit result, I will be predisposed to preserve my mouth close about them." It also can moreover take longer than you found for us to manner and express our emotions absolutely. When we are dysregulated, we can also want to pause conversations and cross lower back to them later. It is our responsibility to talk this, as well as to maintain our promise to transport decrease returned to the talk. However, it's far beneficial if you do now not press us to talk whilst we are activated.

We want assist being inclined. It may be extraordinarily uncomfortable and even terrifying for an avoidantly linked person to enjoy their human vulnerability. Their records has satisfied them that the ones desires will not be met, so they will be decided to break out that feeling. Of route, vulnerability is an essential a part of intimacy. On our forestall, we want to artwork to unlearn the fear of vulnerability. On your detail, growing a steady environment for us to exercising vulnerability, so long as it is also steady for you, can help us in mastering this new ability set.

Yes, we want time and place to ourselves, but this is about us, no longer you. Generally, avoidants regain a sense of protection thru self-regulation. Allowing us time and area to ourselves can help us assemble the trust we need to connect. Given enough on my own time to construct protection, avoidant attachers can (and do) grow to be more comfortable in relationships and desire more intimacy—looking after ourselves allows us to show up in our relationships as extra present and wholesome. Early communique approximately expectations regarding time spent together and aside can assist manipulate every person's goals—or can help you understand if a capacity romantic courting is a mismatch.

We're quite sensitive to complaint—real and perceived. Many avoidants are scared of being "incorrect," of trying our toughest and though failing. While "being sensitive to complaint is wholesome," avoidantly connected people may be greater dysfunctionally sensitive to criticism after they don't trust they're lovable despite the fact that they're wrong. If a person wants to provide feedback to someone who is avoidant, they want to find out nonthreatening settings for the communication, together with sitting next to each exceptional or going for a stroll. When it entails expressing your issues, using "I statements" and finding not unusual ground can assist preserve the communique from devolving proper right into a squabble.

It is honestly sincerely worth repeating: In the give up, us avoidant humans are chargeable for our personal boom.

As formerly stated, a supportive relationship can go an prolonged manner in the direction of assisting avoidants sense more snug and trusting with intimacy, however, the actual art work lies with us. And, as with most self-improvement endeavors, accepting ourselves is the first step in the direction of recovery our attachment. It's vital for avoidantly linked humans to recognize that, effective, there can be a need for a bit more distance from humans, however this is first-class. You don't must punish yourself for it.

That's how I'm dealing with my attachment: allowing it to be the muse that it's far even as additionally coming across new strategies to answer in relationships—a way that calls for plenty of workout. And feeling more deeply understood and receiving compassion from others goes an extended manner within the route of offering me with the safety to obtain this.

Chapter 3: How To Overcome Avoidant Attachment

If you located yourself analyzing your personal manner of existence on this e-book, do not be disheartened. There are procedures to help you mitigate the harm completed as a infant.

Although we can provide the ones 4 guidelines, you can need to be looking for the assistance of a intellectual fitness expert. They assist you to in navigating the maze of emotions that has held you captive since youth.

One, write down pleasant affirmations and take a look at them aloud to yourself on a regular foundation. Positive affirmations do not need to be lengthy phrases; they can be as simple as "I'm lovely" or "I'm profitable, and I'm enough."

The reasoning within the again of studying incredible affirmations to yourself is to update the vintage comments you found approximately your self as a infant. These awful tapes are constantly playing within the historical past of your mind, reinforcing the rejection you felt as a infant. By reading these affirmations aloud, you are changing antique statements with new ones.

Two, learn how to be your very non-public cheerleader. People with an avoidant attachment fashion have been criticized and rejected in infancy, at the equal time as our attachment style became forming. Cheering yourself on and complimenting yourself reinforces the reality which you do now not deserve best awful complaint.

Positive self-speak reinforces the fact that you deserved appropriate statements lower back then and that you deserve effective, setting ahead messages now.

Statements like "I can acquire this" and "I actually have what it takes" spoken aloud to your self will assist you have a more optimistic view of your self as an individual. Positive self-talk may also assist you connect with others. This bonding takes place due to the fact you revel in better approximately yourself, which affords a basis upon which you may construct your records of what others want.

Even if you don't agree or don't forget what you are pronouncing in your first-class self-talk earlier than the entirety, the blessings will come. If you stay with it, those new prophecies about your self will begin to come actual.

Three, hook up with your self using a replicate. This is probably the maximum hard part of the art work to triumph over avoidant attachment fashion. However, the way is easy. You best want a reflect and a quiet room a long way from prying eyes.

Once you are inside the the the front of your photo, start the manner via the usage of telling your self how loads you without a doubt love you. You also can will let you understand which you take delivery of as proper with to your capability to obtain your dreams in existence.

you can discover yourself wracked with giggles earlier than the entirety, but via way of way of persevering with to inform your self remarkable stuff while looking into your eyes, diffused modifications will start to rise up. As you beef up the ones great messages, your conduct and expectancies of others will exchange.

The premise is straightforward. You did not get preserve of the terrific messages from your mom which you required as a infant to experience steady and desired.

Because your primary caregiver did not meet your needs, your emotional fitness suffered.

This lengthy-unhappy emotional want is met with the beneficial aid of talking to your self while searching into your eyes and saying, "I love you."

In effect, you turn out to be your mother, imparting yourself with the emotional assist you have normally wanted.

Four, art work collectively together with your inner baby via visualization. Children typically growth a steady attachment style through interacting with caregivers who keep and guide them as they develop. These intimate moments between mom and toddler create a reservoir of reminiscences for the child, now an person, to draw on at the same time as they'll be distressed.

Those with an avoidant attachment style didn't collect the interactions from their mothers that they required to accumulate their reminiscence reservoir. Because of this lack of care, the ones avoidant adults looking for the consolation of partners and friends at the same time as they will be worrying or otherwise distressed.

Making recollections now could be one way to counteract the outcomes of adolescence neglect about of our emotional goals.

To create particular memories, you should get in contact with the little little one that lives inner all humanity. Making proper reminiscences can incorporate going someplace to entertain your inner child, which incorporates a park, or imagining your self playing on a seashore or in a meadow.

Introduce your self in your inner infant and pay attention to what he or she is announcing about how they sense and what they need. Tell the a part of you that by no means grew up which you're the person version of that baby and understand them for assisting you get this an extended way in life.

If you spend enough time with that little tyke who lives in your soul, you may discover ways to love them as despite the fact that they have been a child out of doors of yourself. When you do, you could have witnessed a miracle. Instead of being the needy individual who is determined to discover someone to fulfill you after which feels trapped, you can find out which you love yourself and are consequently sufficient.

After all, you're that inner infant. To love him or her is to enjoy who you have been and are these days.

How To Date A Person With An Avoidant Attachment Style

1. Communicate with phrases, no longer tantrums

Perhaps it drives you nuts while he does now not contact you for a whole day. You may additionally end up agitated as you consider huge range down the mins until he responds, prompting you to blow up his cell cellphone (triple dip text every person?) or send a passive aggressive message. When you're in this stressful, envious country – do now not have interaction! Get into a rustic of calm through meditating or exercise to get rid of the angst and strain chemical substances. Whatever you do, do not preserve messaging on the identical time as you're disturbing or in a low-vibe country. This electricity is felt; you are no longer fooling anybody with a satisfied face emoticon. When you have got self-soothed and gotten yourself in a powerful temper, make time to speak your wishes and alternatives for your accomplice. Communicating in a wholesome, character manner approach not making desires or looking for to manipulate or put into effect conduct with ultimatums (that is a positive manner to supply an avoidant jogging inside the opposite path).

When you talk your want for connection and conversation without attacking, you each can come up with movement objects a great manner to satisfy your desires for connection similarly to his needs for area and freedom. For example, the next time he feels the urge to "skip poof" into his mancave, he can allow you to recognise that he's taking a few time off and will respond the next day. Because you have got were given negotiated this earlier of time, you will understand it’s nothing private, or a threat to the connection. Of route, he received't be able to modify his conduct to address all of your emotional triggers if you sway extra traumatic. However, the greater solid you're to your attachment, the tons tons less you may take it in my view when he is taking region.

2. Practice staying electricity when he pushes you away

Avoidants enjoy secure whilst their independence or autonomy is not threatened, so if he withdraws, apprehend that it isn't a signal of rejection. For some time, he could likely go through cycles of having close to after which retreating. A pursue-withdraw dynamic happens on the identical time as one man or woman actively pursues the opportunity's feelings on the equal time as the opposite withdraws out of worry of exacerbating the state of affairs. If this dynamic persists for an prolonged time period, it is able to be tremendously bad to a dating.

This dynamic, but, may be altered thru recognizing every special's underlying needs in battle conditions. If your avoidant partner is not prepared to speak approximately his or her emotions and calls for private location, be affected person and deliver it to them; pushing or pressuring them will most effective motive them to withdraw more.

3. Look at his intentions

You can also feel hyper-vigilant, intensely tracking your partner's emotions and especially touchy to cues that your accomplice is pulling away, especially if you are an worrying kind. However, leaping to conclusions motives you to misinterpret each different's emotional kingdom, that would result in unnecessary battle and strife. Take a second to hold in thoughts your companion's intentions earlier than reacting. Then, in advance than you decide, accumulate more records and proof. When you postpone your initial worry-based totally totally responds, you may be amazed at how an entire lot less hard it's far to accurately understand the state of affairs. Learn how to distinguish between your interpretations and assumptions and the data of the scenario. Perhaps he's preoccupied with artwork and isn't always thinking about communication. This does now not propose that the relationship is in jeopardy. Looking at the records and his intentions will let you advantage perspective and avoid falling into an emotional spiral.

four. Pick sports as dates

Avoidants are at risk of getting out of place of their heads and overthinking topics. So spend quality time together doing sports activities like hiking or strolling, or maybe attempting out a modern sport. He'll be much more likely to loosen up and display you affection if he is present and inside the 2nd on the equal time as you bond and be part of. The extra you bond, the more vasopressin and oxytocin are produced – the bonding chemical materials accountable for rapport and consider.

five. Support, Not Fix

One of the maximum tough stressful conditions for avoidants is spotting and discussing their very non-public emotions. Significant studies, but, indicates that really naming our feelings is critical in diffusing and coping with them. Psychologist Dan Siegel calls this method "naming it to tame it." "Emotions are handiest a form of strength, continuously seeking out expression," he says. And the first step in expressing them is to discover the right words. Encourage your partner to mag, with a view to assist him hook up with his feelings rather than disconnect from them. However, be careful now not to preference your accomplice's increase more than he does. If he isn't always interested in growing and taking component to transport ahead, you have to each acquire him as is or flow on. If his avoidant attachment style is causing you a terrific deal of ache, you need to recollect whether or not a extra consistent companion might be a better lengthy-time period in shape for you.

6. Avoidants, in conjunction with you, want and want love.

A amazing frame of studies suggests that avoidant attachment is the give up end result of mother and father who have been overly controlling, smothering, or unresponsive to their infant's wishes. Do now not pick out or disgrace a person who has an avoidant attachment fashion; their early youth studies stressed out their connection to intimacy in a manner which often reasons them extraordinary loneliness. They suppress their attachment tool subconsciously, which they're regularly unaware of doing.

While dating a person with an avoidant attachment style can also moreover appear hard, the pleasant news is that with assist from their accomplice and their private self-art work, they may be able to development from avoidant to everyday. When they understand they'll be stable and that intimacy will no longer control or reason them the same pain they skilled as children, a extra healthful narrative becomes reaffirmed through the years and experience, and that they often rewire their baseline.

Chapter 4: How to Increase Communication

1. Be affected person

Change is viable, but it is able to not rise up in a single day.

Your accomplice has determined out that avoidance is essential for survival.

It is essential to provide them time to learn how to specific themselves in techniques that have been previously risky for them to carry out that.

2. Create an surroundings of protection

Your avoidant companion may additionally additionally have values and concept strategies that alter from yours. Understanding their point of view allow you to discover common floor.

Accept your partner as they're if the least bit possible. When they enjoy solid to be themselves, your functionality to talk and degree of intimacy will decorate.

three. Respect cultural versions

If your associate comes from a tradition wherein human beings don't percent their feelings, he or she may additionally moreover precise their feelings in one of a kind methods — and that is fine. Inquire about how they would love you to precise your emotions to them.

You may also moreover discover it useful to investigate every one of a kind's love language, as they will place one-of-a-kind portions of price on the following kinds of connection than you do:

Words of confirmation

Quality time

Physical touch

Acts of issuer or practical assistance

receiving offers

4. Try to understand how they view 'desires'

As kids, avoidant partners in all likelihood had to learn how to appear plenty a lot much less "needy" that permits you to preserve caregivers spherical. As a end end result, your companion might not explicit their dreams, and they will be confused if you do. People in their international are predicted to take care of themselves. They enjoy wonderful humans and revel in relationship, however they do no longer understand the idea of mutual dependency. With this statistics, you could try and increase your guide network and, at instances, self-soothe.

five. Avoid controlling their behaviors

Not feeling supported or verified can be frustrating. In mild of this, try to resist the urge to manipulate their actions if you want to satiate your desires because of the truth it'd backfire.

Because they'll be aware about having plenty independence, avoidant partners additionally have a tendency to be sensitive while feeling controlled thru using others.

6. If possible, provide on my own time

Healthy obstacles are the foundation of any a fulfillment relationship.

Avoidant companions frequently require a few by myself time each day, which may be a source of shame. It can help them revel in extra standard if you beat them to it and provide the time by myself first.

Saying some element like, 'hello, why do not you spend a while in the park after lunch and I'll go do my private problem for a piece' ought to lead them to experience confirmed for his or her solitary dispositions.

7. Try not to break their region

Avoidant companions might also moreover have spent most in their formative years on my own, so they will become absorbed of their paintings, responsibilities, or pastimes. When you walk in and begin talking, it could take them a moment to modify. They may additionally seem startled or irritated.

You may discover it beneficial to:

Not call their name from some other room

Not interrupt them inside the center of a go along with the glide

offer a transition length from being by myself to being social

8. Consider some social sports that don't involve them.

If the least bit viable, avoid pressuring your accomplice to do a little factor they may be not cushty with. Do not try and pressure them to participate in social sports sports with others if they do no longer need to. Give them the choice to participate on the identical time as furthermore giving them the selection to move away within the event that they grow to be uncomfortable.

9. Clarify dreams for bodily contact

With an avoidant partner, physical affection and intercourse can be wonderful. Some avoidant partners can be uncomfortable with bodily contact. They may additionally dislike lengthy hugs or enjoy unsure about not unusual touch.

Let them realize you understand that they have got first rate options. Then inform them you want to find out a middle floor where you can sense linked a number of the time via contact even as they may be capable of experience comfortable in their very private pores and pores and skin and now not feeling beaten.

10. Communicate approximately your sexual wishes

While you are courting, an avoidant companion can also have a fashionable intercourse stress, however they'll lose interest over the years and like time by myself. It may be useful to speak approximately your very non-public sexual options collectively along with your accomplice to be able to better apprehend one another.

11. Try now not to take rejection in my opinion

There may be instances at the same time as your accomplice isn't always sexually, emotionally, or physical available. Take a deep breath and keep in mind that this isn't always because of you.

If you take their propensities for my part and accuse them of not worrying about you, they may revel in shame and need to distance themselves from you.

12. Prioritize the use of I-statements

Better relationships are built on powerful communique. If in any respect feasible, try to unique your feelings with out being accusatory. When you're taking obligation for the manner you feel or what you're going through, you do away with the blame out of your companion.

Instead of announcing "you hurt me and made me experience unimportant even as you did now not respond," an "I" declaration might be "I felt hurt and unimportant as soon as I did no longer get a reply."

thirteen. If possible, talk when you’re calm

Try to speak approximately troubles at the same time as you are not concerned in a problem. When every of you're calm, it's far thousands easier to deal with issues.

14. Try to keep away from grievance

When your companion does some component you need, praise them and attempt to keep away from criticism. Complaints popularity on precise behaviors, even as grievance gets to the coronary heart of who your companion is as an character.

15. Try phrasing court instances as requests

Asking your partner to begin performing some thing in preference to asking them to save you will result in a greater tremendous interplay. If you need them to forestall doing a little aspect, inform them what you need them to do as an alternative.

Instead of criticizing them for being now not capable of determine on a eating place, you can say, "I locate it impossible to resist at the identical time as you select out the restaurant we visit."

16. If they take a look at out, resume the communique later

Your avoidant companion might also furthermore struggle with emotional conversations. When you communicate feelings, they'll turn out to be overwhelmed.

You may additionally furthermore locate it useful to wrap up if you be aware:

pressure or anxiety

“looked at” facial expressions

zoning out

Request that the verbal exchange be persisted later so you can unique your desires.

It is useless to hold talking to an avoidant man or woman when they have reached their limit because it triggers their fear of being held captive and dominated.

17. Consider a compromise

Avoidant companions frequently see troubles as a win-or-lose scenario. Remind them that compromise is an option. This permits them to apprehend that their point of view is valued within the interaction.

For instance, you may say, "I would really like to maintain arms in public, but I apprehend we can also need to compromise."

18. Validate their feelings

Validate your accomplice's emotions after they select to specific them. You do now not need to endure in thoughts how they experience, however you have to be given that their emotions are valid in the same manner that yours are.

19. Ask how they feel

Your avoidant associate can also avoid expressing their wishes for fear of performing needy. Probing a piece and making sure they are telling you what they in truth want can help them sense cherished for who they may be.

For instance, you could ask, "Is this film surely k with you?" I need you to be happy and not experience which includes you gave in ."

20. Consider operating with a couples therapist

If your partner has avoidant character ailment or avoidant tendencies, you do no longer want to try this by myself.

Couples counseling may be incredibly useful.

It assist you to and your companion not handiest boom intimacy and improve communique, however it may moreover help you understand every different's views and research.

Chapter 5: The Anxious-Avoidant Dance

Few people may also recollect pain to be a gift.

To be clear, relational trauma/abuse isn't always earned, need to no longer be pursued, and isn't being repainted in a woo-woo, outstanding mild right right here. In retrospect, pain becomes a gift in the planned constructing of a tale over time that gives us a enjoy of redemption from an vintage story of grief or blame. In the present, ache signs us to issues and can point us within the direction of answers. Repeated pain—the proper same sensation felt again and again—can turn out to be a revelation, bringing a experience of control and a danger to break loose from an agonizing pattern.

When you Google "poisonous dating" or "stressful-avoidant lure," you could discover one precise relational pattern that couples therapists see so regularly that it could experience cliché—a pattern this is deceptively invisible whilst you are within the midst of it. Beneath the usual issues—cash, mess in the home, time manage, the manner to region the youngsters—lies this relatively not unusual pattern.

Many humans stay in worlds that our companions cannot see, worlds which is probably driven by means of manner of way of abandonment or oppression. We are each suffering to transport towards others, asking them to relieve our feel of abandonment and alter our our our bodies, or we are fighting to stability self and other, unsure a manner to unite without dropping self, knowing that when on my own, we're capable of feel each on my own and physically regulated. The most avoidant among us, even as perhaps giving up on the possibility (or dissociating from it maximum of the time), although crave connection outside of self.

When the ones opposing extremes collide, it could be electrifying. The little one in a single sees the opportunity and, on a few unconscious diploma, says, "There is a steady man or woman." Now I'll be cared for. Now I can loosen up." the kid within the different says "There is a few different toddler, like me, any man or woman who will not control me," I'll be secure now."

However, as quick as a positive degree of intimacy and dependence is reached, the individual that desires to enjoy cared for starts offevolved offevolved to feel abandoned, and the person who desires to keep away from oppression realizes they have got re-created their early life. They've observed however some different man or woman who can't meet their wishes, any other who isn't always truely tuned in and is as a substitute distracted via their personal panic, perpetuating the oppressed's belief: "I'm on my own." I want to be self-sufficient. I can't depend on my partner." So they may withdraw and resentfully say, "Take care of your self." "I haven't any preference." And so the dance starts offevolved.

The profiles of "opposing" attachment patterns proven underneath represent extremes. Life is hardly ever as clean or as black-and-white as any ebook. We all keep notable traumas in specific natural vessels, and we internalize the worldviews of numerous attachment figures (along with caregivers or mother and father circle of relatives, friends, or own family; partners; and therapists) in the end of our lives.

The Abandoned: Mobilized and struggling to reconnect

Attachment fashion: Anxious/preoccupied.

Mission: Draw attention. Restore connection. Find constant safety.

Post-battle reminiscence formation: Gathering great proof about the connection to use as protection in competition to abandonment.

Those who believe they had been deserted are more likely to obsess over dating troubles specially else.

They may be much more likely to acquire out, entice (or name for) hobby, or maybe create drama a good manner to elicit a desired response from others—a reaction that, whilst furnished, has nowhere to land. They may additionally trying to find reassurance whilst appearing not able to pay attention it.

Self-abandoned in instances of immoderate emotion, many aren't able to absolutely have interaction in gift-second interactions. This creates a form of brief-circuit that, specially in times of panic-driven assault, perpetuates a cycle of struggle and helplessness for all activities involved.

Outside of struggle, folks which is probably annoying make a contribution plenty-favored electricity to the relationship.

They are commonly better at speakme (or as a minimum more willing), and that they use that position to carry greater social motion into any relationship, stopping their companion from turning into remoted (despite the fact that their avoidant associate may combat them on this). They are also inclined to visit any period to keep the connection intact. They also can moreover undergo any blame for relationship problems—blame and judgment that their avoidant accomplice deflects as it feels too risky to bear. The oppressed associate deflects, while the deserted accomplice catches willingly.

In the abandoned-oppressed partnership, the demanding (deserted) feature serves because of the fact the inhale: strength up, enthusiasm and play, conflict of words.

Those who are demanding often see themselves as pursuing love "the way love is meant to be": by no means forsaking each specific, sharing the whole lot, and in no manner being by myself.

Main cause: Obtain great attention and preserve outside relationships.

Stuck vicinity: Gives up self results that allows you to hold right away to some other. Rumination without a witness equals self-abandonment.

Triggers: Partner disengagement, partner interest on a person else, associate lack of energy/initiative, communique inconsistencies (associate says "I love you" with a easy expression), or popular lack of accomplice interplay.

Experience: Inability to self-soothe, experiencing inner abandonment, projecting that onto the world honestly so it seems to be taking region anywhere.

The Oppressed: Immobilized and hoping for Safety (Alone), Permission (Relationship)

Attachment fashion: Avoidant/dismissive.

Mission: Hide and hold. Stay small and keep away from punishment. Present as low- need /low-call for. Wait for freedom (with resignation and resentment).

Post-struggle reminiscence formation: Gathering had evidence approximately the relationship to apply as deflection even as caught.

If a hidden virtual camera is set up within the domestic of an oppressed-abandoned couple, they will take a look at a dramatic difference in behavior even as the oppressed accomplice is on my own. Many human beings do now not recognize how a ways a person on the avoidant (oppressed) component of attachment will visit preserve their anonymity. They can also just close to the curtains greater frequently, walk softer, communicate in a quieter voice, smile to elicit protection, or stay clean-faced to avoid engagement. They would probably certainly talk much less or maintain extra factors in their lives non-public. Many will prepare dinner after their associate or roommate has lengthy gone to mattress. Some may additionally furthermore refuse to pay their mobile phone bills as a manner to keep away from arguments and "legitimize" their loss of reaction or communique. Some may also moreover exaggerate their paintings schedules in preference to sincerely asking for by myself time. They may additionally study for decrease-stage jobs that hold them out of the spotlight, or they will turn out to be "pushed" at art work, walking continuously to show themselves and keep away from judgment. They may additionally additionally say "I love you" whilst they may be in truth dissociated from any emotion, due to the truth they're aware of dissociation as a manner of existence, and it's miles a good deal less complicated for them to placate others than to stand struggle and "waste time."

To be honest, the initial rush of unseen motion is sometimes absolutely getting the to-do listing finished as fast as feasible (with out an audience) in advance than returning to a greater subdued country and feasible self-law.

Time is regularly precious in this prevent of attachment, partially because the character lives a half of of-life, hibernating in the presence of others. If the deserted side is frightened of abandonment, the oppressed thing accepts it as reality, believes they are by myself, without enough manual or sources to live on, and is green with envy of people who ask to percentage their already constrained assets. From the outside, self-sufficiency is preferred. There isn't always any perceived desire for the avoidant. It's a herbal reaction to a international wherein want have become both forbidden or outright punished.

On this facet of attachment, there is usually a terrific conservation of belongings—a planned and monitored rationing of time, space, budget, and so forth. This is self-sufficient, unsupported existence, with its accompanying experience of shortage and fatalism—a frozen combination of giving up and putting on, no longer taking dangers, not committing to something long-time period, even hoarding what little is held. At the extremes, the ones on the avoidant element are normally professional at self-denial and rationing, and they may be regularly green with envy of a associate who seems greater frivolous—a associate who lives a hint more carefree, as though there is guide available inside the international, as if there isn't always steady judgment and anger pondered inside the worldwide.

Those on the oppressed component are regularly raised in houses wherein feelings aren't contemplated, so that they live attuned to loss of attunement from others, occasionally subconsciously hoping their partner might probably word at the identical time as some thing is incorrect so it might not must be spoken. Even if the selection for assistance is severe and lifelong, asking for assist feels too inclined. Behind all of the blaming, deflecting, and nondisclosure is an intense worry of oppression and rejection—a perception that talking with a partner is equal to giving that accomplice a weapon. Asking an avoidant individual how they may be feeling can effortlessly be interpreted as entrapment.

Individuals who lean on avoidant techniques are normally right listeners—every so often willingly, every now and then resentfully—used to setting their private wishes apart to present for others. They are actually respectful of space and boundaries, and companions frequently rely upon them for balance. They may be quite attuned to their accomplice's dreams, pleasant them without the associate asking or noticing—modeling the shape of attunement they would like for their accomplice, and then blaming their partner for now not noticing.

When there can be no war, the oppressed (avoidant) position serves as the relationship's exhale: strength down, soothing, resignation/elegance ("allow it relaxation"), renew, repair, get higher, maintain (which includes ongoing calculations of to be had time and electricity and clarifies the draw to the electricity possessed with the aid of those greater disturbing).

Those at the avoidant factor see themselves as realistically pursuing relationships, believing that everyone is by myself, that secure dependence does not exist, and that everybody need to deal with their very very own desires and feelings so that you can avoid burdening others.

Main cause: Avoid terrible interest even as maintaining inner enterprise enterprise.

Stuck vicinity: Detachment from hurtful additives method little decision or integration, similarly to little alternate in relationships (every internal and outside).

Emotion suppression may be framed as self-oppression (judgment, manage, forget about approximately of emotion).

Triggers: Any risk to scarce assets along side time, money, or place.

Animal-degree physical indicators—angry or disapproving faces, voices, amount—are also a cause, as they threaten safety and autonomy.

Experience: Feeling internal contempt and projecting it out into the world, making it seem like happening anywhere. Anger and disdain for the area also imply rejection/abandonment. While felt for quick intervals, abandonment is frequently suppressed via way of dissociation and/or inner judgment/contempt, with messages which encompass "dollar up and be difficult."

The Dynamics of the Dance

The dance is hard and acquainted to all involved.

The oppressed aspect acknowledges in an aggravating one of a kind the equal strength that it suppresses in self: the helpless, stressful toddler. While to begin with inquisitive about that electricity out of kinship, avoidant strategies try to suppress/oppress that strength in the annoying associate as properly. '

Initially inquisitive about their avoidant partner's protection and seemingly steady hobby, the disturbing aspect ultimately realizes they may be dropping the extreme love they skilled inside the beginning while their accomplice modified into so without problems enamored. This reasons extra panic and more fight for interest. To the avoidant factor, which is already searching for signs of oppression, the aggression in that panic seems like manipulate. Disdain grows for the deserted, heightening the worrying panic and avoidant withdrawal.

This dance could not very last if every side felt secure in intimacy. When matters grow to be too near and comfortable, the traumatic aspect stops pursuing, wondering, and might sabotage. At the very least, there can be some manipulate over while the "inevitable" abandonment takes region. When matters end up too far off, the avoidant has been mentioned to update processes, even taking on the pursuer role. Between the techniques of each extreme, a tolerable diploma of intimacy/distance is maintained.

Chapter 6: Ending The Anxious-Avoidant Dance

The battle is each a battle for and a protection in competition to intimacy.

If we are capable of most effective preserve others as tightly as we've got held ourselves, we are capable of gravitate in the route of others who have a similar capacity for internal pain—people who are at a similar distance from strong attachment. Clinging and retaining off are strategies for retaining a consistent distance from intimacy. While we may additionally additionally dislike our companion's technique, we additionally depend on it. We are inquisitive about it.

The Never-Ending Conflict

The abandoned side is pronouncing: "If they might simply stay and reassure me, I may be calm in a minute,"

The oppressed factor is saying: "If they might clearly stay calm and prevent attacking, I might be able to remain gift with them."

We change states as war techniques.

The number one elements required for attachment reenactment are dependency and struggle. When we acquire a positive diploma of intimacy in a courting—at the equal time as we begin to depend emotionally on a companion—the relationship starts offevolved to deal with a modern-day form. This new shape pretty similar to our relationship with one or greater number one attachment figures. The stressful factor research an pressing, bodily activating coaching for abandonment within the 2nd, on the identical time as the avoidant facet studies oppression, trapped, loss of potential to transport, incapacity to pick out their personal lifestyles—every craving and resigned.

Extremes polarize. If one aspect relaxes and movements in the route of the middle, the alternative follows in form. This dance can be ended with the aid of the use of either character. And that popularity vanishes in the midst of organic survival reactions. Living in baby states, we react now not to our companions, but to our caregivers, to the embodied memories of our caregivers.

The Self-Perpetuating Loop

It every now and then seems like we are trapped in a role. Each individual plays a sequence of cued reactions which may be so nicely-rehearsed and particular that they'll have been written in a script.

The avoidant aspect is self-aware however lots tons much less professional at speaking internal activities (thoughts, sensations, and feelings) to others. The disturbing factor communicates higher but is masses much less aware about internal sports, a whole lot much less able to meet and talk them objectively without becoming stuck up within the physical activation of feelings.

Conflicts on this relational pattern have a propensity to be longer and much less powerful. One facet becomes the pursuer, amplifying to benefit notable hobby, even as the opportunity turns into the distancer, disengaging to avoid terrible hobby—a in no manner-finishing retraumatizing dance.

The avoidant side desires much less preventing, says they can not be found in war, and makes use of abandonment as a weapon, a tool ("the silent treatment")—the exquisite factor their accomplice can concentrate. The demanding facet says they feel like they'll be taking walks on eggshells, and can't depend upon their accomplice to be emotionally present usually, (anger, volume). Each side feels left out, invalidated, and unacceptable (often perceived as a confirmation of the equal feelings felt in childhood).

Fighting styles are regular with attachment patterns and survival techniques.

Those who are irritating have a tendency to make bigger, land clearly in emotion, call for help, and can be much more likely to combat physical, notwithstanding the truth that the touch is "small," which Incorporates pinching or blocking a path of get away. These "minor" attacks can become extra essential over time.

Those on the avoidant thing are much more likely to decrease, freeze, land as far some distance from the emotion as possible, or maybe dissociate. They may additionally moreover stay inflexible, stoic, and inexperienced with envy, wishing their companion ought to "get it" and prevent the assault, therefore breaking the freeze. ("Don't they see how trapped and helpless I am?") They combat in a good buy less visible strategies, that might often experience manipulative, invalidating, and "insane" to the greater direct demanding element. They can also furthermore deflect, placate, or maybe gaslight their partners with a purpose to reclaim their freedom and self, to re-set up manage over their our bodies as they break out reputedly infinite and fruitless battle.

Grieving the Fantasy of the Perfect Union

Both elements on this dance are full of delusion and fear, and they each need their accomplice to satisfy them in a selfless way—to meet their emotions with ideal attunement and empathy, and to help them calm their our bodies.

The favored situation is only to be had in the location of 1-sided attachment (this is, decide-little one dating). While it could appear in treatment, it's far neither romantic nor lengthy-term outdoor of the remedy room. A healthful romantic dating necessitates inner connection and popularity, in order that companions are not predicted or preferred to act as mother and father—to satisfy an prolonged-unmet want.

Romantic relationships are inherently bidirectional in nature. Each difficulty shares control in an man or woman romantic courting and each is responsible for their personal boom, speaking their wishes, making alternatives approximately the connection, and finding motive and resource out of doors of the relationship further to inside it. The relationship turns into stagnant if each partner stops developing on their very own. If one associate will become overly reliant at the opportunity, resentment can boom, and the relationship can become careworn and tumultuous.

Healing Approaches

In courting, some of the healing can arise in the way we meet our companions:

For the avoidant facet: Be privy to your companion's stressful assumptions. Recognize their need for reaction... And reply. This is the essential relationship trade: bid and respond. Inquire for and acquire interest. While it could appear smooth, it is a protracted manner from it. Without it, the relationship will perish over the years. Concentrate on retaining regular connection due to the truth this is wherein their wounding came about. And this can set you off.

For the worrying component: Be privy to your associate's avoidant strategies and perceptions. They are absolutely as legitimate as your fear. If your accomplice calls for time to update to humans mode, ask nicely for that switch within the next ten minutes or hour, and placed yourself in a function in which they might come to you in desire to you drawing close them (which seems like a danger and gets equated with manipulate)." In particular phrases, emphasize their sense of agency and freedom, recognizing their wholeness and the proper to choose out their private life (despite the truth that those picks seem insignificant within the grand scheme), because of the truth this is in which their wounding passed off. If you could display that you recognize their valid, separate goals and which you're not forced or harmed with the aid of the usage of them, they may sense commemorated and safe to like you.

Individually, a superb deal of the recuperation is about reputation and ownership, about gaining knowledge of to be and stay with every inner emotion, to fulfill it with moderate compassion, using the equal heat eyes you'll use to satisfy a infant or an cherished home canine. In the ones moments while you appearance back through your own family's generations and observe these relational/emotional patterns playing out, live with those moment. Feel it in your body. Honor the actual and cutting-edge-day experience of a racer who has been exceeded down a generational baton and has nowhere to head.

If you are on the stressful element, Be aware that your research have taught you to recognition more outwardly on the same time as ignoring what goes on internally. This is the supply of loneliness and panic. You can also not enjoy by myself if you could be every with and separate from your inner disappointment. (This calls for workout and, in a few times, the assist of a therapist.) A yoga or mindfulness practice also can be beneficial.) Maintain your hobby about your private internal enjoy in addition for your companion's. Before beginning a verbal exchange, check your frame. Practice taking note of each yourself and your companion on the equal time. If you experience you have not any sources outdoor of your courting, recognition on growing new pursuits and social connections -something to dispel the perception that this relationship is "the whole lot." Notice how smooth it's miles as a manner to take shipping of the blame your partner deflects towards you. Consider that.

If you are at the avoidant side, Be aware that your beyond stories have taught you to hold subjects to yourself and to surrender even as your belongings are stretched. Try doing the alternative. When you are stuck, skip spherical and speak about your day—even the additives you located will bore or burden your partner. And, on occasion, are trying to find help. Experiment. See what takes place whilst you lean into your associate, final inclined on all tiers. Recognize that panic lies underneath dissociation. Find a constant area to feel and device your panic (gardening, nature, your partner, a pet, or some trouble your chosen aid is).

Break Up or Continue On?

This dating can art work, if every events:

Accept obligation for their personal attachment desires and techniques.

Accept duty for the continuing paintings of each self-growth and relationship increase.

Remain open to test constantly with techniques to meet each self and one-of-a-kind.

Discover strategies to get right of entry to an internal domestic base and witness inner ache.

And, in the long run, as opposed to staying in the courting out of fear; because of the fact a accomplice fills a lacking capacity set; through the use of the usage of default to maintain reputation quo and preserve strength; due to the truth the intimacy in reaching the straight away of breaking up is actually too excessive; or because of the reality the ache of rejecting your partner (generally ache in you which you mission onto them) feels endurable (every now and then forcing dissociation on the concept of cut up), apprehend this courting doesn't want to paintings. By the time each companion has processed their adolescence traumas and are available to look this dance for what it is, the prevent of this sample may also moreover sense flawlessly everyday.

When we grieve what changed into lacking—at the same time as we prevent fighting in opposition to the reality of it and the reputedly unbearable emotion of it—we're now not interested in the identical cycle. Some human beings find out that the attachment trauma grow to be the pleasant factor that they had in commonplace, that they needed to come collectively to heal each awesome, and that they will be content material with the concept of parting methods and sending love. Some see it as a critical lesson or a new edition of themselves that they needed to "hurt into."

From the mindset of natural increase, the elements people that are looking for out this pattern accomplish that for a purpose. If we've were given been no longer capable of "be with" our ache—if we've got got inherited or developed "man or woman" identities that abandon or assault the elements of ourselves that harm—then the consistent reenactment of relational patterns pushes us again into opportunities to meet the ache, to meet the child inner us, to in the long run see it with superb eyes, and to recognize what that difference certainly manner. It is as although our internal infant is pronouncing, "This! Right right here! THIS IS WHAT I FELT: the feelings, the sensations on your body, the urge to panic or flee: THIS IS WHAT I FELT! For some years! This modified into actual. This came about. No one noticed. See me. Be with me. Meet me how I'd want to be met."

The gift of remedy is that this: arriving at a factor wherein each the breakup or continuation feels wholesome for both events, in which each thing believes on a physical level that they're accurate sufficient, that the story makes revel in, that closure has been found, and that anyone is privy to a way to flow beforehand with gentle compassion for every self and special.

Chapter 7: Avoidant Attachment Key Characteristics

Attachment styles have a deep affect on structuring our interpersonal connections, impacting how we connect to humans emotionally and in element. Avoidant attachment, one of the maximum critical attachment sorts located in attachment precept, is characterized with the useful aid of a dread of closeness, emotional unavailability, and a choice to preserve emotional distance from others. Understanding this attachment type is vital as it sheds moderate on complex human behaviors and feelings, giving a blueprint for private improvement and healing.

At its root, avoidant attachment comes from early stories in infancy and adolescence, whilst caregivers might also moreover were inconsistently present or conscious of the kid's emotional desires.

As very last outcomes, people with avoidant attachment commonly normally have a tendency to extend a deep-seated dread of rejection and abandonment. To address the ones concerns, humans installation a protection mechanism that drives them to keep away from emotional connection and vulnerability in their adult relationships.

One of the primary capabilities of avoidant attachment is emotional detachment. People with this attachment kind normally war to talk their emotions definitely. They also can reduce price the fee of emotional connection, considering it as a signal of inclined factor or fragility. Consequently, they will have trouble developing and maintaining deep relationships, due to the fact actual emotional connections are normally abandoned in want of self-reliance and independence.

Another trait of avoidant attachment is a dread of reliance. Those with this attachment kind commonly discover it difficult to rely upon others, specifically in times of want. They are uneasy with the concept of relying on a person else for emotional guide, believing that this reliance may also result in disappointment or rejection. Consequently, they prefer to repress their emotional wishes, setting up a mask of self-sufficiency and detachment.

Avoidant human beings are frequently prone to dismissive perspectives towards relationships. They can also moreover have a pessimistic attitude of affection and backbone, feeling that obtaining too near a person might really result in tragedy. This distrust typically arises from earlier situations once they enjoy deceived or allow down with the aid of way of important people. Consequently, they will come to be emotionally aloof and casual, undermining doubtlessly exquisite relationships earlier than they have a danger to bloom.

Addressing avoidant attachment is of vital significance for numerous motives. Firstly, understanding one's attachment type is vital in stopping the sample of unfavourable partnerships. By records the patterns related with avoidant attachment, people may gain perception into their behaviors and emotions, setting up the direction for healthful connections with others. Awareness is step one toward transformation, permitting humans to confront their shielding structures and try inside the direction of developing greater steady and profitable relationships.

Secondly, addressing avoidant attachment has significance for non-public properly-being. Avoidant women and men often undergo a robust sensation of loneliness and isolation manner to their dread of intimacy. Confronting and jogging via the ones anxieties can also purpose better self-recognition and self-popularity, developing a deeper experience of identification and self confidence. This, in flip, may additionally additionally additionally beautify well-known lifestyles satisfaction and intellectual well-being.

Addressing avoidant attachment is vital for breaking down emotional boundaries. The disability to communicate feelings freely no longer simplest impairs non-public relationships but moreover impedes personal improvement and self-discovery. By know-how and going through avoidant inclinations, humans may additionally engage on a remodeling course in the route of emotional honesty. This calls for learning to really accept vulnerability, precise real feelings, and create empathy and compassion in the path of oneself and others.

In the context of romantic relationships, controlling avoidant attachment is crucial for building successful partnerships. Intimate partnerships increase on mutual get hold of as right with, emotional intimacy, and open conversation. Avoidant humans, restricted thru their attachment style, generally fail to create those crucial inclinations of a connection. By resolving their avoidant tendencies, people may establish a greater sturdy emotional basis, allowing them to take part in relationships with sincerity and openness.

Attachment styles are generally exceeded down from parents to youngsters, generating a cycle of insecure connections. By breaking a long way from avoidant behaviors, humans can also create a more being involved and safer surroundings for his or her kids, fostering the development of better attachment styles within the next generation.

Breaking Walls, Building Bridges: A Journey Through Avoidant Attachment

In the silent recesses of my reminiscence, there lurks a story—a story of a pal who, like masses people, wrestled with the cryptic maze of avoidant attachment. Sarah changed right into a smart character, brief-witted and appealing, however below her beautiful smile, there was a veil of detachment that she wore like armor.

Growing up, Sarah had discovered to be fiercely impartial. Her dad and mom, on the identical time as properly-that means, were emotionally aloof, their love disguised within the back of a wall of stoicism. As a outcome, she grew up negotiating existence's limitations on my own, her feelings frequently confined to the quiet recesses of her heart. This early placing produced the template of her attachment style—a mosaic of self-reliance, dread of closeness, and a careful avoidance of emotional vulnerability.

Sarah’s tale isn't an isolated one. Many humans, at a while in our lives, have felt the frost of avoidant attachment. It's like recognition getting ready to a crowded birthday celebration, witnessing the exuberant festivities from afar however now not capable of sign up in in. For Sarah, forging bonds became like treading a tightrope; the priority of falling, of getting too near, made her movements careful and calculated.

I don't forget a specific event at the same time as Sarah confided in me. We sat beneath a sky protected with a tapestry of stars, the sector regarded large and infinite, but our hearts had been heavy with the weight of human feelings. As she spoke, her terms held the echo of many souls who had danced alongside comparable threads of separation.

"I need to feel near human beings," she stated, her eyes reflecting the moon's lovely brightness. "But if a person strategies too cautiously, I experience myself taking flight. It's like an instinct, a safety mechanism that I can't control."

In that second, I determined now not certainly Sarah, however a reflect of the numerous those who deal with the nuanced subtleties of avoidant attachment. Her fight became no longer simplest a private conflict but a not unusual narrative of trying connection some of the stronghold of emotional shields.

Through her narrative, I diagnosed the fee of empathy—the bridge that unites hearts throughout the span of human reviews. It become this empathy that driven us to find out the depths of avoidant attachment collectively. Through shared tales, tears, and laughter, we started disposing of the limitations that had stored her coronary coronary coronary heart guarded for good-bye.

Sarah’s story have emerge as a monument to resilience and the electricity of human connection. Slowly, with care and compassion, she started out chipping away on the barricades shielding her coronary heart. It wasn’t smooth; there were disappointments and durations of unbearable vulnerability. Yet, with each stride beforehand, she realized the transformational energy of allowing herself to be visible, warts and all.

In sharing Sarah’s tale, my goal is to acquire out to all people who, like her, have skilled the alienating tendrils of avoidant attachment. Your combat isn't in vain; it’s a testimonial to your electricity. Just as Sarah discovered peace within the embody of understanding pals, there may be a community of empathy equipped to cradle you too.

Behind the terms on those pages are hearts that sympathize collectively along with your ache, brains that realise your issues, and souls that enjoy your achievements. Together, allow us to rip down the bounds of avoidance and accumulate bridges of connection, one emotional story at a time.

Chapter 8: Defining Avoidant Attachment

Avoidant attachment, a center term in attachment concept, delineates a sure manner of responding to others, set up profoundly in early youngsters studies. Understanding avoidant attachment desires digging into its numerous layers, comparing each its distinguishing traits and the formative research of younger people that deliver rise to this attachment type.

Avoidant attachment, frequently referred to as as an insecure-avoidant attachment, is described via the usage of an person's inclination to avoid emotional connection, intimacy, and reliance in relationships. Those with this attachment kind monitor a robust choice to maintain emotional distance from others, frequently due to a fear of rejection, abandonment, or being ate up via the desires and emotions of others.

This distancing tendency is a coping approach shaped in response to caregivers who have been unevenly responsive, emotionally unavailable, or invasive for the duration of the man or woman's youth.

Beginnings and Early Development: Avoidant attachment owes its beginnings to the vital length of infancy and early teens, a time at the same time as the foundations of emotional relationships and interpersonal take delivery of as authentic with are constructed. During this age, newborns rely on their caretakers not simplest for bodily nutrients however moreover for emotional stability and validation. For a child to shape a strong bond, consistent and responsive being worried is crucial. However, in conditions of avoidant attachment, caregivers generally fail to deal with the children's emotional goals frequently.

Children with avoidant attachment normally come across caregivers who are emotionally unavailable or dismissive in their emotional shows. These caregivers may additionally additionally moreover restrict indicates of vulnerability or emotional reliance, unwittingly suggesting to the child that their wishes for consolation and reassurance are undesired. In such conditions, the teenager learns to push aside their emotional symptoms and longing for connection as a survival tactic.

Avoidant attachment can be a outcome of numerous parental practices, including rejecting a toddler's efforts to are looking for for consolation, delivering inconsistent solutions to their suffering, or showing ache with emotional indicates. These early encounters amplify within the teenager a enjoy that counting on others for emotional manual effects in unhappiness and rejection. Consequently, the youngster adjusts with the useful useful resource of restricting their emotional demands and avoids searching for comfort from caregivers.

As the child matures, those early attachment styles get internalized, affecting their perceptions approximately themselves, others, and relationships. Avoidant parents, regardless of regularly searching self-sufficient and ready, have deep-seated anxieties of connection and vulnerability. The avoidance of emotional connection turns into a default reaction, inhibiting the building of sturdy and profitable relationships in maturity.

Understanding the complicated interaction amongst early reports and the formation of avoidant attachment is top. It gives insights into the complicated emotional panorama of individuals showing this attachment style, organising the manner for compassionate treatments and strategies focused at growing strong attachment relationships and recovery preceding traumas. Dissecting the motives of avoidant attachment, we may additionally assist clients on a remodeling direction within the route of growing greater wholesome, greater private relationships primarily based on accept as proper with, emotional openness, and true mutual expertise.

The Impact of Avoidant Attachment on Adult Relationships: Navigating Communication, Intimacy, and Trust

Avoidant attachment, firmly ingrained in young adults activities, casts a big shadow over man or woman relationships, affecting the way human beings view and take part in private ties. Examining its affect on communique, intimacy, and consider exposes a complex tapestry of problems that folks with avoidant attachment confront, frequently impeding the appearance of profitable and sturdy relationships.

Communication: Communication, the lifeblood of each dating, bears the burden of avoidant attachment's impact. For people with this attachment kind, expressing feelings freely is normally a difficult undertaking. They pick out to underestimate the importance of their sentiments, questioning that vulnerability can bring about rejection or engulfment. As a end result, their conversation fashion becomes careful, buried in vagueness, and usually lacking in emotional intensity.

Avoidant people may additionally conflict with expressing love, comfort, or maybe primary gratitude, unknowingly developing a hollow in their relationships. Their dread of emotional connection can also moreover moreover result in a addiction of indirect verbal exchange, in which their real sentiments are veiled beneath a mask of detachment.

This indirectness from time to time fosters misunderstandings and infection, making it hard for their companions to recognize their real emotions and needs.

Intimacy: Intimacy, each emotional and bodily, is a victim of avoidant attachment. The worry of proximity and vulnerability inhibits the set up order of profound emotional ties. Intimate moments, full of believe and vulnerability, turn out to be elusive, as avoidant women and men reflexively withdraw as closeness tiers increase. Their deep-seated worry of reliance and rejection every now and then hinders them from virtually collaborating within the intimacy-building technique.

In romantic relationships, this worry of intimacy can also moreover end up an aversion to physical contact, issues in discussing personal thoughts and emotions, and an unwillingness to completely take part in times of emotional connection. As a consequence, relationships with avoidant humans may moreover lack the emotional depth and closeness which are wanted for their lengthy-term preservation and evolution.

Trust: Trust, the middle of each precise relationship, is dramatically broken thru avoidant attachment. Individuals with this attachment type find it tough to accept as true with others, often because of in advance tales of uneven being worried and emotional unavailability. Their worry of dependency and possIble disappointment makes it difficult for them to clearly receive as real with that their companions will supply their emotional needs or reciprocate their feelings.

This loss of agree with can also motive a chronic cycle of suspicion, in which avoidant folks are unwilling to dedicate emotionally in relationships, fearing betrayal or desertion. Their guarded temperament may additionally unknowingly weaken the accept as authentic with of their partners, who may perceive their emotional distance as indifference or loss of determination.

Reflecting on Your Attachment Style

Recognizing Avoidant Patterns Within

Take a minute to go deep in the depths of your coronary coronary heart and inspect the styles that govern your relationships. Reflect on your emotional reactions, your problems, and your dispositions in private interactions. Do you find out yourself careful to open yourself to others? Are you careful approximately leaning on a person emotionally? Do you frequently are trying to find independence in your relationships, even on the sacrifice of intimacy? These may be signs of avoidant attachment subtly affecting your relationships.

Let me percentage a tale that would relate on your very own critiques. Meet Emily, a energetic and incredible younger woman, who seems self-confident in all regions of her lifestyles besides for her sexual connections. She found herself completely unattached, traveling from one short-lived dating to some other. On the floor, she appeared sturdy and self-sufficient, however underlying the masks turned into a profound dread of emotional vulnerability.

Emily's relationships determined a predictable pattern. At the onset, she can be excited and engaged, playing the earliest levels of attachment and connection. However, at the same time as the relationship grew and emotional expectancies installation, she may want to routinely reduce lower lower back away. The dread of being too dependent on her husband, along side a first rate difficulty with expressing her actual feelings, drove her to bring together emotional distance.

Eventually, her enthusiasts may additionally hit upon her emotional detachment and the relationships might collapse, leaving Emily feeling solitary all once more.

Emily's enjoy is handiest one of the severa times of the way avoidant attachment may additionally moreover quietly impact our love existence. By noticing these dispositions internal ourselves, we take the first step inside the route of information our attachment style and its impact on our relationships. It's now not an smooth avenue; self-mirrored photograph commonly involves addressing our darkest fears and insecurities. Yet, it's far on this mirrored photograph that we discover the critical component to unlocking better, more worthwhile partnerships.

Imagine a life wherein emotional connection doesn't motive tension, in which take into account comes effects, and wherein you may take shipping of vulnerability with out fear. This is the promise that includes figuring out and treating avoidant attachment. It's now not about blames or self-grievance; it's about knowledge ourselves in the most thorough way possible.

As you reflect in your private attachment style, preserve in mind the following questions:

What are your first memories of emotional reference to caretakers or important others?

How do you react to emotional closeness to your gift relationships? Are there sports at the identical time as you routinely retreat or create distance?

Do you discover it hard to talk your emotions simply, particularly in instances of vulnerability or distress?

In instances of dispute, do you prefer to keep away from addressing your mind or wishes, deciding on quiet or emotional detachment?

Reflect on your former relationships. Are there repeated types of emotional detachment or issues in preserving intimacy?

By in reality answering these questions, you set up the framework for great self-discovery. Remember, know-how your attachment type is not approximately identifying yourself but alternatively approximately getting belief into your emotional surroundings. It's about knowledge the difficulties that might be inhibiting your ability to make deep, sizable relationships and jogging in the course of overcoming them.

Chapter 9: Key Indicators of Avoidant Attachment

Understanding your attachment style is a pivotal step within the route of self-attention and private increase. To help you on this adventure of self-discovery, I've crafted a questionnaire that will help you confirm the important problem symptoms and signs and symptoms of avoidant attachment. Please mirror on every query thoughtfully, considering your beyond and current-day relationships. Be honest with yourself, as this honesty might be your guiding mild within the direction of a deeper expertise of your attachment style.

Instructions: For each declaration, charge how frequently it applies to you on a scale of 1 to 5, in which 1 shows "Not the least bit real for me" and 5 shows "Very genuine for me."

I find out it tough to accept as true with others truely, especially in romantic relationships.

1 2 three 4 five

I frequently downplay the significance of emotional intimacy in relationships.

1 2 3 4 five

I determine on to handle my issues and emotions by myself, without seeking out useful aid from others.

1 2 three 4 5

I am uncomfortable with an excessive amount of bodily or emotional closeness with others.

1 2 three four 5

I fear becoming too counting on others for emotional useful resource or comfort.

1 2 3 4 five

I frequently find it difficult to particular my proper emotions, specifically if they may be awful or inclined.

1 2 three four 5

I price my independence pretty and every now and then prioritize it over my relationships.

1 2 3 four 5

I have a tendency to suppress my emotional wants to keep away from being a burden to others.

1 2 3 four five

I simply have a records of brief-lived relationships, and I discover it tough to keep prolonged-time period commitments.

1 2 3 four five

I often feel uncomfortable at the same time as my associate expresses strong emotions, specifically if they're horrible.

1 2 three 4 five

Scoring:

10-20: Low danger of avoidant attachment tendencies.

21-30: Mild warning signs and symptoms of avoidant attachment patterns; self-mirrored picture and growth possibilities gift.

31-forty: Moderate signs and signs and symptoms of avoidant attachment; preserve in thoughts exploring techniques to deal with those styles.

41-50: Strong warning signs of avoidant attachment; searching out guide and interventions can be fairly useful.

Reflect on your ratings and bear in thoughts the patterns that emerge. Remember, this questionnaire is a tool for self-reflection, not a definitive analysis. If you discover that your ratings mean a bent within the direction of avoidant attachment, be compassionate with your self. Awareness is the first step within the route of alternate, and with willpower and useful resource, you could embark on a transformative journey closer to building healthier, more solid relationships.

Reflecting on Past Relationships: Identifying Avoidant Attachment Patterns

Take a minute to open your mag, a sanctuary in your thoughts and feelings. In this location, we are capable of have a test the tapestry of your previous relationships, searching out the sensitive threads that might display patterns associated with avoidant attachment. This hobby is not about assigning blame or that specialize in preceding wounds; it's about understanding your emotional reactions and relationship behavior. Here are some guidelines to assist your mirrored image:

Describe Your Past Relationships: Reflect to your most critical relationships, every romantic and platonic. Write approximately the parents you were engaged with, the dynamics of the relationships, and the emotions you professional. Take some time to seize the essence of every courting, which includes its origins, peaks, and very last ends.

Explore Your Emotional Responses: Dive into your magazine with honesty and openness. Explore your emotional reactions in a few unspecified time within the destiny of these connections. Did you discover it hard to specific your feelings overtly? Were there activities while you straight away removed yourself emotionally? Reflect at the feelings that arose within the course of disagreements or instances of closeness.

Identify reoccurring Patterns: As you write, look for reoccurring patterns. Are there comparable topics or behaviors that developed at some stage in multiple relationships? Perhaps a propensity to retreat at the same time as disagreements erupted or a trouble of counting on your partner emotionally. Identifying these patterns is crucial considering they frequently contain the critical factor to know-how your attachment type.

Consider the Endings: Reflect at the ends of your previous relationships. Were there tendencies in how the ones partnerships concluded? Did you find out it difficult to dedicate, ensuing in breakups? Or did you have got were given a incredible enjoy of consolation at the same time as relationships ended, displaying a fear of intimacy? Examining the endings might offer beneficial insights into your avoidant attachment patterns.

Explore Childhood Influences: Think decrease returned to your younger humans and early interactions with caretakers. Were there instances were your emotional desires were not noted or unmet? Reflect on how the ones early events need to have affected your thoughts about relationships and intimacy. Understanding the origins of your attachment kind ought to likely display your cutting-edge behavior.

Consider Your Partner's Responses:

Reflect on how your partners reacted on your emotional clues and distancing strategies. Did they display displeasure or confusion? Or did they seem to conform in your emotional patterns? Consider how your avoidant conduct should have altered the dynamics of the relationship and your companion's emotional tales.

Remember, this writing interest is a exceptionally personal exam. It also can need to reason excessive emotions, and that's clearly natural. Allow yourself the room to revel in and reflect. The styles you discover aren't designed to outline you but to empower you with self-recognition. With this data, you may flow into on a road of recovery, installing higher relationships constructed in trust, emotional intimacy, and right connection.

Chapter 10: Exercises for Attachment Reflection

Emotions are the threads that weave the complicated material of our relationships, and know-how them is crucial to treating attachment issues.

At the center of my personal journey through avoidant attachment, there got here a 2d of deep knowledge, an awakening to the electricity of addressing emotions and anxieties.

I notably preserve in mind an afternoon whilst an brilliant buddy, a person I really relied on, asked a easy question: "What are you feeling proper now?" It regarded like a sincere question, but it felt like I had to decide out a difficult puzzle. I paused, the simplicity of the inquiry contrasting dramatically with the maelstrom of feelings interior me.

At that moment, I decided to deal with my issues head-on. I closed my eyes, took a huge breath, and allow myself experience. It turned into unsightly, unnerving even, as layers of buried emotions began out to emerge. Fear, fear, a experience of unworthiness—those emotions, lengthy buried underneath the pretense of avoidance, surged to the floor like bubbles in a protracted-forgotten pond.

Tears welled in my eyes as I desired the ones sentiments. It end up a raw, willing 2d that I had purposefully averted for years. But some of the tears, there has been moreover a gleam of remedy. For the primary time, I have grow to be addressing my emotions in choice to escaping from them.

Through this come upon, I determined out that studying feelings and anxieties isn't best approximately tackling the unsightly; it's about embracing the complete kind of human experience. It's approximately accepting pleasure, love, and pleasure along fear and grief. In doing so, I changed into gradually deconstructing the limitations of avoidance, brick via the use of brick.

When you have interaction in the ones wearing activities, hold in thoughts that addressing your emotions and problems is a powerful act. It's a voyage into the depths of your psyche, in which you stumble upon the very forces which have not unusual your attachment fashion. It acquired't generally be clean; in reality, it can be quite tough. But inner this studies lies the call of the sport to statistics your self, mending your traumas, and putting in place a path inside the course of safe, significant partnerships.

May you find out the fortitude to dive into your feelings, tackling your anxieties with a compassionate heart. Just like I addressed my feelings, so can also you. And in this shared adventure, we discover the seeds of trade, flowering proper right right into a existence rich in emotional closeness and right connection.

Exercise 1: Emotion Mapping

1. Create a list of the primary feelings: Start via naming middle feelings which consist of satisfaction, fear, rage, sorrow, love, and humiliation.

2. Reflect on preceding memories: Recall specific conditions out of your beyond at the equal time as you felt each of these feelings within the context of relationships. Note down the incidents, the people involved, and your emotional reactions.

Example: Situation - Family amassing, Emotion - Joy, People - Parents and siblings, Reaction - Laughter, warmth.

3. Identify styles: Examine your list and search for tendencies. Are there superb emotions that usually occur to your relationships?

4. Do exceptional activities routinely provoke effective emotional responses? Understanding those patterns would possibly show insights into your attachment-related emotions.

Example: Emotion - Fear, Trigger - Intimacy, Pattern - Feeling willing and taking flight

Exercise 2: Fear Exploration

1. Identify attachment-related troubles: Write down your fears regarding attachment and relationships. These might also encompass problems of rejection, abandonment, closeness, or reliance. Be as specific as possible.

Example: Fear - Rejection, Concern - Being unlovable, Source - Past romantic courting wherein partner ended the connection all at once.

2. Trace the origins: Reflect to your upbringing and in advance tales to discover the property of those problems. Were there specific conditions or relationships that brought about those fears? Understanding the roots ought to possibly assist you contextualize and cope with them.

Example: Fear - Abandonment, Origin - Childhood trauma, Situation - Parents divorcing, Feeling - Overwhelming fear of abandonment.

three. Challenge your fears: For every worry, positioned out a counter-narrative. Challenge the concern with examples out of your existence even as the concern did not seem or grow to be disproven. This exercising may help you set up a more balanced view of your anxieties.

Example: Fear - Closeness results in rejection, Counter - Close friendship wherein vulnerability have end up favored and reciprocated.

Exercise 3: Visualization and Reimagining

Find a quiet vicinity: Sit or lie down in a peaceful and cushty area in which you received't be afflicted.

Close your eyes: To unwind, near your eyes and inhale deeply commonly.

Visualize a strong courting: Imagine yourself in a courting in which you revel in absolutely cushty, cherished, and loved. Picture the encounters, the emotions, and the recollect. Hold onto this photograph and immerse yourself inside the sensations associated with it.

Example: Visualize - Sitting with a companion, giggling collectively, feeling absolutely installed and loved.

Explore your emotions: While envisioning this sturdy connection, pay attention to the feelings that rise up. Are there sentiments of heat, delight, or pleasure? Acknowledge and embody the ones emotions.

Reflect on the versions: Compare those suitable feelings with the issues and anxieties you've observed earlier than. Consider how the feelings in this vision vary out of your attachment-associated anxieties. Reflect on what it'd take to bridge the space between the ones excellent feelings and your present emotional evaluations.

These physical sports are designed to be chronic exercise. Revisit them on every occasion you sense the want to have a look at your feelings and worries related to attachment.

Strategies for Healing Avoidant Attachment

Breaking a long way from the grips of avoidant attachment is a brave and reworking journey—one which incorporates self-compassion and self-recognition as regular partners.

Imagine a starlit night time, the sector quiet besides for the rustle of leaves within the wind. Under that significant sky, I stood, my coronary heart echoing the vastness of the universe, however feeling remarkably small. I knew that sensation well—it turn out to be the echo of avoidant attachment echoing in my psyche.

There were moments at the identical time as starting up up regarded like reputation on the point of a precipice, horrifying and thrilling in equal diploma. For years, I had felt that my price come to be based absolutely upon my capability to be self-enough, never recognizing the brilliant loneliness that incorporates this self-imposed solitude. Avoidance have emerge as my armor, insulating me from the vulnerability of connection, or so I believed.

Then, in the silence of that starlit night time time, a few element moved indoors me. It come to be a time of incredible self-meditated photograph, a second once I understood that I deserved more than a life of emotional separation. It end up a moment of self-compassion as soon as I decided on to treat myself with the identical love, I may additionally supply a valued pal.

With each step, I discovered the skills of self-attractiveness. I not unusual my defects, spotting that they have been no longer failings but the extremely good mosaic of my humanity. I started out out to speak to myself like I may need to to a close to pal—moderate, supportive, and affected person. Through this self-compassionate lens, I started out to understand my price past the regulations of avoidance.

This course wasn't freed from hurdles. There had been disappointments, instances of hysteria, and periods at the same time as vulnerability seemed like an abyss. But at the ones times, I recalled the starlit night time time time, the moment of self-compassion that had launched me on this journey. With each war, I have grow to be stronger, greater resilient, and strangely, greater connected.

Today, I proportion this story not as a narrative of success however as a reminder. A reminder that self-compassion and self-beauty are not high aspirations however feasible devices internal your maintain close. You, too, deserve the warm temperature of connection, the encompass of records, and the softness of self-love. It starts offevolved offevolved with a 2nd—possibly below a starlit sky, perhaps in the silence of your room—in which you resolve to be your personal pleasant pal.

May you discover the electricity to move in this road of self-compassion and self-reputation, because of the reality inner it lies the call of the game to mending avoidant attachment and embracing a lifestyles entire of love, both for others and, most importantly, for yourself.

1. Understanding Self-Compassion:

Embracing flaws: Recognize that flaws are a common human enjoy. Allow your self the freedom to be wrong without self-grievance.

Practicing Self-love: Treat your self with the identical love and information which you could provide to a close to pal. Acknowledge your troubles and screw ups with loving kindness.

Cultivating Mindfulness: Develop mindfulness techniques to live gift along aspect your emotions. Mindfulness lets you observe your thoughts and emotions with out judgment, establishing a loving mind-set in the direction of oneself.

2. Embracing Self-Acceptance:

Acknowledging Your charge: Understand that your price is innate and not based totally absolutely upon outside confirmation or connections. Embrace the concept which you are well worth of love and belonging exactly as you are.

Letting Go of Perfectionism: Release the unrealistic expectancies of perfection. Accept that mistakes and disasters are a part of the human experience and do no longer lessen your simply really worth as a person.

Honoring Your Emotions: Allow your self to experience a extensive shape of emotions, which incorporates vulnerability and worry. Avoidance of emotions absolutely continues the loop of attachment conduct. Embrace your feelings as critical messengers helping you toward healing.

3. Building Secure Self-Reliance:

Developing Internal Validation: Work on growing self esteem that comes from inner as opposed to trying to find validation from outside resources. Engage in matters that provide you with a feeling of success and pleasure.

Setting Boundaries: Learn to set healthful limitations in relationships. Understand that setting up obstacles is an act of self-care and an critical component of growing healthy relationships.

Practicing Vulnerability: Allow your self to be inclined, both with yourself and honest people. Vulnerability is the doorway to emotional intimacy, permitting actual relationships to thrive.

4. Seeking Professional Support:

Therapy and Counseling: Consider getting remedy or counseling from specialists specialized in attachment and relationships. Therapists can also furthermore offer critical insights, coping competencies, and a supportive placing for restoration.

Supportive boards: Engage with assist organizations or on line boards wherein parents proportion similar critiques. Connecting with people on a comparable course can also moreover bring validation, statistics, and a feel of belonging.

In the approach of recuperation avoidant attachment, realize that transformation takes time and effort. Be patient with yourself, acknowledging the improvement you're making, regardless of how minor it can appear. Embrace the course with self-compassion, embracing oneself as a bit in development. By practicing self-compassion and self-recognition, you not most effective put together the path for mending your avoidant attachment however additionally create the framework for a lifestyles rich in self-love, significant relationships, and emotional pleasure. You are deserving of the affection and know-how you preference, and it starts offevolved offevolved with the deep act of accepting oneself completely.

Nurturing Secure Attachment: Guided Exercises for Embracing Intimacy and Vulnerability

Embarking on the street within the course of a more stable attachment style is a super experience, complete of self-discovery, compassion, and full-size relationships.

There grow to be a time even as the concept of setting out, of being definitely prone, changed into equal to entering into a lion's den. I tremendously bear in mind a time from my personal experience, a second that impacted my outlook on intimacy all the time.

In a modest café, the numerous soothing fragrance of freshly made espresso, I positioned myself involved in a dialogue that regarded odd.

It have turn out to be with a chum I relied on, and but, my palms were sweaty, my pulse raced, and phrases stopped in my throat. The communique went into the place of my worries and insecurities, the very center of my avoidant tendencies. I paused as though the phrases had a weight too huge to hold.

But some difficulty altered at that without delay. Instead of recoiling, I took a big breath and determined directly to percent. I confessed my concerns, my traumatic conditions, and the uncertainties that had tormented me for years. It changed into frightening, like going onto a tightrope with out a safety net. However, as soon as I talked, I felt a experience of launch, an emancipation from the shackles of avoidance that had chained me.

My friend listened, now not with judgment but with information. In that vulnerability, I found out a amazing reality: being open and being really visible, didn't weaken me—it made me stronger. It became a second of connection so uncooked and real that it marked a turning aspect in my lifestyles.

So, even as you begin those sports activities to increase a stable connection, hold in mind this 2nd. Remember that vulnerability isn't always a sign of susceptible factor; it's miles a testimonial to your electricity. Every time you open your self, every time you permit your self to be visible, you are taking a step in the direction of liberation.

It is probably terrifying, it is able to be hard, however inner that vulnerability is the opportunity for exquisite recuperation and connection.

May you find out the strength to include those sports activities, to stroll into the ache with the eye that, on the opposite element, there may be the hazard for real connection, understanding, and the deep, fascinating relationships you deserve. With every exercising, with every second of vulnerability, you're recuperating your energy and rewriting your narrative.

1. Embracing Self-Compassion:

Personal Love Letter: Write a love letter to your self, appreciating your strengths, resilience, and the unique attributes that make you who you are. Celebrate your adventure, appreciating the hurdles you have conquered. Keep this letter near and assessment it whenever self-doubt is to be had in.

Daily Affirmations: Start your day with awesome affirmations. Affirm your deserving of love, belonging, and satisfaction. Repeat strains like "I am worth of affection simply as I am" and "I consist of vulnerability as a power." Repeat the ones affirmations in the route of the day, specially finally of intervals of self-doubt.

2. Building Trust and Vulnerability:

Vulnerability diary: Create a diary devoted to your inclined instances. Reflect on moments even as you allowed yourself to be open and sincere, although it appeared unsightly. Write about your sentiments, the responses you bought, and any useful outcomes. This workout emphasizes the concept that vulnerability also can result in significant relationships and understanding.

Shared Vulnerability: Engage in vulnerability drills with a depended on buddy or associate. Share a private worry or insecurity and percentage the manner it feels to explicit it freely. Witnessing reputation and empathy from others ought to likely gradually redesign your revel in of vulnerability.

three. Strengthening Emotional Bonds:

Sympathetic Listening: Practice sympathetic listening together with your own family. During interactions, deal with genuinely data the opportunity man or woman's emotions and opinions. Validate their sentiments without judgment. This exercise builds empathy, builds emotional relationships, and presents a normal environment for open speak.

Thankfulness regular: Establish a thankfulness ordinary for your relationships. Express thank you for the easy, big moves that your family provide. It is probably a pleasant remark, a beneficial gesture, or a 2d of actual connection. Acknowledging and appreciating those times will increase your emotional connection and fosters receive as real with.

four. Mindful Connection:

Attentive Presence: Practice attentive presence to your interactions. Put aside distractions, installation eye touch, and certainly take part in the present. Mindful presence promotes deeper relationships, helping you to revel in the richness of shared recollections.

Breath of Compassion: In times of self-doubt or worry, workout the "Breath of Compassion." Take prolonged breaths, envisioning yourself breathing in love and splendor and expelling self-criticism and worry. This soothing technique fosters self-compassion and allows you confront vulnerability with a compassionate coronary coronary heart.

Every time you try to be open and permit human beings get near you, it is an remarkable trouble. Be affected individual with yourself and function an extraordinary time at the same time as you do some element even a chunk bit brave. By training these gadgets, you're constructing strong relationships which are probably complete of affection and information. Your adventure is unique and you've got the power to make superb, strong friendships.

Chapter 11: Crafting Your Personal Growth Action Plan

Steps to Overcome Avoidant Attachment and Foster Healthier Relationships

Not good-bye within the past, I determined myself at a crossroads, wrestling with the heavy load of avoidant attachment. Relationships, as quick as a supply of satisfaction, have emerge as a maze of emotional distance and anxiety. It become at one specifically emotional duration of self-contemplated picture that I found out it grow to be time for exchange.

I quite take into account sitting down with a pen and paper, exactly as you'll be doing now. I became resolved to layout a plan for my personal development, a route out of the labyrinth of avoidance. It wasn't easy; the pen felt heavy in my arms, weighted down via way of the usage of years of self-doubt and uncertainty.

But as I began out setting down my objectives, I remembered a chat with a chum who had formerly had comparable annoying situations. Their narrative have become my guiding mild. They described how, little by little, that they had determined out to lean into ache, take transport of vulnerability, and cultivate their self-worth. Their avenue wasn't sincere; it grow to be a succession of youngster successes and espresso screw ups. Yet, with each failure, they located the fortitude to upward push up yet again, bolstered via self-compassion and a vision of healthy relationships.

I, too, selected to pursue this street. My non-public development movement plan have come to be a mosaic of self-compassion, remedy, and incremental publicity to vulnerability. It includes every day affirmations to growth my arrogance, treatment intervals to untangle deep-seated troubles and practical moves to exercising openness in my relationships. Each day, I reminded myself of my buddy's tenacity, locating concept from their course.

Through those practical attempts, I started out detecting minor variations. Moments of actual connection started changing the emotional easy I had become used to. It wasn't a quick metamorphosis, but a consistent blooming of my actual self, unburdened with the aid of manner of avoidant tendencies.

As you gather your personal improvement movement plan, understand which you aren't on my own. Just like I determined braveness in my friend's story, you can discover idea in the reminiscences of others who have battled and conquered avoidant attachment. Your roadmap can be particular and relevant in your studies and goals, but the endpoint is the equal: a existence filled with safe, being concerned connections and a strong feeling of self esteem.

I choice you expand as a good deal as be robust, kind to yourself, and don't forget in yourself. Every time you take a look at some issue new or strive some element hard, you're making your story higher. You are changing from being scared to being brave and from not liking subjects to loving them. As you change, you could have unique friendships and relationships in that you enjoy satisfied and related.

To lead you in this remodeling street, I invite you to assemble a tailor-made motion plan. Consider the following degrees as a basis to your non-public person direction closer to restoration and developing solid connections:

1. Self-Reflection and Awareness:

Daily Journaling: Dedicate time every day to report your mind and feelings. Reflect to your interactions, triggers, and instances of vulnerability. This method promotes self-popularity, bringing important insights into your attachment styles.

Therapeutic Support: Consider treatment or counseling. A mental fitness expert also can deliver specialised recommendation, assist, and coping abilities, expediting your recovery path.

2. Cultivating Self-Compassion and Self-Acceptance:

Daily Affirmations: Start your day with self-compassionate affirmations. Remind yourself of your benefit of love and splendor.

Mindfulness & Meditation: Engage in mindfulness and meditation sports activities to promote self-focus and self-compassion. Regular mindfulness physical sports activities can also additionally assist you continue to be gift, minimizing challenge approximately destiny connections.

three. Building Emotional Literacy:

Emotion Identification: Practice spotting and categorizing your emotions. Use emotion charts to growth your emotional language and increase your capacity to articulate emotions.

Empathetic Listening: Practice lively listening with others. Understand their emotions, viewpoints, and requirements. Building emotional intelligence creates empathy and deepens relationships.

four. Developing Healthy Communication Skills:

Peaceful Communication: Learn and exercise non violent communique capabilities. Focus on expressing your needs and feelings assertively on the equal time as empathetically know-how others' views.

I-Statements: Use "I" statements to hold your thoughts and wishes without blaming or criticizing others. For example, say, "I experience worrying when I experience emotional distance" in desire to "You normally make me worrying."

five. Challenging Avoidance Through Gradual Exposure:

Modest movements: Gradually project your avoidance with the aid of creating modest actions. Initiate a brief, inclined speak with a trusted buddy or partner. Celebrate the ones moments of bravery, no matter the quit quit result.

Self-Compassionate Reflection: After every sensitive touch, reflect to your emotions and evaluations. Acknowledge your courage, no matter the response. Self-compassion bolsters your resilience.

6. Building Secure Relationships:

Limits: Set easy and healthful limits to your interactions. Communicate your wishes and respect the limits of others. Boundaries offer a sense of safety and predictability.

Mutual Respect: Seek relationships primarily based on mutual respect and information. Nurture relationships with those who apprehend your feelings, understand your vulnerabilities and reciprocate your attempts for closeness.

7. Practicing Patience and Persistence:

Cultivating Patience: Understand that private development requires time Be affected man or woman with yourself, knowing that setbacks are regular.

Embrace those times as possibilities for gaining knowledge of and improvement.

Self-Compassionate Reflection: Regularly mirror in your improvement. Celebrate your triumphs, regardless matter number their duration. Acknowledge your efforts toward improvement and admire the tenacity internal you.

Creating an motion plan focused in your specific instances permits you to overcome avoidant attachments and set up better connections.

Chapter 12: Inspiring Success Stories

Allow me to introduce you to Inspiring Success Stories of people who've bravely navigated the complexities of avoidant attachment and emerged a hit, fostering stable and pleasurable relationships. These memories feature beacons of preference, illuminating the transformative energy of self-reflection, resilience, and the unwavering notion inside the opportunity of trade.

1. Sarah's Journey to Emotional Intimacy:

Sarah, as soon as entrenched inside the types of avoidant attachment, released right into a adventure of self-discovery. Through remedy and self-reflected image, she determined to find out her avoidance triggers and face them head-on. With everyday effort and the guide of her therapist, she practiced vulnerability in small, viable steps.

Sarah's strength of mind paid off when she discovered the braveness to explicit her private fears and wants to her accomplice. Through affected person information and open verbal exchange, Sarah and her companion constructed a relationship grounded in take delivery of as proper with and emotional intimacy.

Today, they have amusing the satisfaction of actual connection, proving that overcoming avoidant attachment is certainly possible.

2. Mark's Transformation Through Self-Compassion:

Mark's avoidant tendencies added about a chain of quick-lived relationships, leaving him feeling remoted and unfulfilled. Through self-compassion practices, which includes daily affirmations and mindfulness sports activities, Mark started out out out to venture his terrible self-perceptions.

As he found out to embody his vulnerabilities with kindness, his worry of intimacy often diminished. With newfound self-beauty, Mark entered right into a dating in which he felt robust enough to unique his feelings overtly. Through the gentle steering of his accomplice and the strength he placed inside himself, Mark professional the warm temperature of real connection, proving that self-compassion is a powerful catalyst for exchange.

three. Emily's Triumph in Building Trust:

Emily, scarred thru the use of past opinions, struggled with remember troubles that permeated her relationships. Through treatment, she explored the origins of her avoidant attachment and the underlying fears that hindered her capability to bear in mind. Emily practiced placing boundaries and speakme her needs openly. With the help of her therapist, she worked on reframing her beliefs approximately trust and relationships. Slowly, Emily commenced to permit her protect down, permitting herself to recall her associate. Through consistent attempt and the affected man or woman expertise of her loved ones, Emily's once-fragile bear in mind transformed right right into a solid basis for lasting relationships, illuminating the path for others going thru comparable struggles.

These stories display us how strong and succesful people may be. By gaining knowledge of about themselves, being kind to themselves, and dealing with their fears, the ones human beings had been able to alternate their lives for the better. They confirmed us that it is possible to move from being afraid of having near others to having healthy and loving relationships. Their recollections encourage us to absolutely receive as right with that we're able to make our very personal relationships better too, and that we deserve love, accept as genuine with, and closeness.

Chapter 13: Understanding Avoidant Attachment

Exercise 1: Exploring Your Attachment Style

Consider your attachment style for a moment. How do you generally method relationships? Are you greater snug with independence and self-reliance, or do you normally commonly generally tend to are searching for closeness and connection? Write down your preliminary thoughts and observations approximately your attachment fashion.

After trying this workout, sit down quietly and allow any feelings that upward push up to be present. Take a deep breath and remind yourself that self-discovery is a courageous act of private increase. Embrace any insights that come to you and hold them lightly to your coronary heart.

Exercise 2: Reflecting on Childhood Experiences

In this workout, we delve into the memories and stories of your early life that might have brought on your attachment style. Take some moments to reflect for your early years. What form of connections did you have got were given together with your primary caregivers? Were they responsive and nurturing, or did they appear faraway and unavailable?

Write down any big reminiscences or feelings that ground inside the course of this contemplated photograph. Remember to be compassionate with yourself as you discover those sensitive regions. If essential, take breaks and pass again to the exercising on the equal time as you experience geared up.

After completing this workout, take time to honor your inner infant. Offer phrases of consolation and reassurance, acknowledging any ache or unmet goals that rise up. Engage in self-care sports activities that bring you pleasure and nourish your soul.

Exercise 3: Identifying Attachment Triggers

Reflect on situations or conditions that trigger emotions of soreness or a preference to withdraw emotionally. These triggers can fluctuate from one person to the next. Notice if tremendous behaviors or situations generally tend to evoke an avoidant response inner you. Write down these triggers and explore the underlying feelings associated with them.

After figuring out your attachment triggers, bear in mind wholesome coping mechanisms you may rent whilst confronted with them. Practice self-soothing strategies, which include deep breathing, meditation, or venture sports activities that convey you a experience of calm and grounding.

Exercise 4: Examining Relationship Patterns

Take a second to take into account everyday subject topics or dynamics which you have noticed in past or current relationships. Do you commonly have a tendency to distance your self emotionally? Do you find it tough to believe and speak in confidence to others? Write down your observations with out judgment.

After finishing this workout, mirror at the impact of these patterns in your essential properly-being and the outstanding of your relationships. Consider the changes you would love to make and the new courting dynamics you preference to domesticate.

Cultivating Self-Awareness

Exercise 1: Mindful Self-Reflection

Locate a serene region wherein you can sit down without problems. Take a couple of deep breaths on the identical time as remaining your eyes. Set your mind relaxed and awareness on the winning 2d. Begin to mirror on your mind, feelings, and sensations with out judgment.

During this exercise, permit your thoughts wander and explore various factors of your existence and relationships. Notice any regular patterns or issues that emerge. Be curious and compassionate towards your self as you delve into your internal panorama.

After your conscious self-reflection, take a few moments to write down any insights or observations that arose. Remember, self-reputation is a powerful device for non-public increase and transformation.

Embrace the newfound expertise you have got received.

Exercise 2: Journaling Your Emotions and Reactions

Pull out a easy piece of paper, your journal or write in the place provided beneath. Set a timer for 10-15 minutes. Start writing freely, permitting your feelings and reactions to flow onto the net net web page. Explore the way you sense about severa factors of your relationships, attachment, and any annoying situations you have got were given encountered.

Do not fear about grammar or shape. This is an possibility to allow your inner voice be heard. Let the terms pour out with out judgment. Pay hobby to any everyday topics, styles, or emotions that get up all through your journaling consultation.

Afterward, reread what you have got written. Take word of any substantial insights or shifts in angle. If you enjoy snug, proportion your reflections with a trusted buddy or therapist who can offer steering and help to your adventure.

Exercise three: Mapping Your Attachment Triggers

Create a visible map of your attachment triggers. Write "Attachment Triggers" within the circle in the subsequent web page. Then, draw traces extending from the middle circle, representing one of a type triggers you've got got diagnosed.

Label each cause on its respective line. Reflect on situations, behaviors, or phrases that evoke emotions of pain, tension, or the urge to withdraw emotionally. Be as particular as viable in figuring out your triggers.

Once you have were given finished your map, take a 2nd to examine the connections amongst wonderful triggers.

Notice any patterns or common problems that emerge. This visible illustration will assist you benefit a clearer statistics of your triggers and their impact on your attachment style.

Exercise 4: Recognizing Avoidant Defense Mechanisms

Explore the protection mechanisms you'll be inclined to lease while confronted with emotional intimacy or vulnerability. Reflect on beyond evaluations and be aware the way you normally reply. Do you locate your self becoming emotionally far off, keeping off conversations, or shutting down?

Write down the protection mechanisms you understand inner your self. Be compassionate as you renowned the ones coping techniques you superior to protect your self. Remember that they served a reason inside the past however may now not serve you in cultivating healthy relationships.

After recognizing your defense mechanisms, keep in mind possibility tactics to reply. Explore more healthful coping techniques, which includes open communiqué, practicing vulnerability in small steps, and searching for manual from trusted people. Embrace the braveness to mission and cross past these protection mechanisms as you go with the flow closer to steady attachment.

Take a moment to mirror in your experience with the ones self-attention physical video video games. How did aware self-reflected photograph, journaling your emotions and reactions, mapping your attachment triggers, and spotting avoidant safety mechanisms affect your know-how of yourself and your attachment style?

Chapter 14: Rewriting Limiting Beliefs

Exercise 1: Identifying Negative Self-Talk

Take a second to tune into your inner speak. Pay interest to the mind and beliefs that rise up whilst you face demanding situations, come upon setbacks, or engage in self-reflected picture. Notice any negative self-talk that emerges.

In this exercise, write down the horrific self-talk you regularly pay attention to your mind. Be sincere and compassionate with yourself as you find the ones limiting ideals. Acknowledge that those thoughts do now not define you but are patterns that can be modified.

After identifying your horrible self-talk, take a deep breath and provide yourself kindness and information. Remember which you have the strength to task and remodel the ones ideals.

Exercise 2: Challenging Negative Beliefs

Once you've got have been given identified your awful self-communicate, it's time to project those ideals. Take every terrible belief and observe the evidence supporting it. Consider whether or not or now not there are any opposing viewpoints or examples that disprove your proscribing assumptions.

Write down the evidence in competition to every horrible notion, supplying examples from your personal research in which viable. Embrace the opportunity to reframe your thoughts and open your self as much as new possibilities.

After tough your horrific ideals, replicate on the brand new insights and views you have got were given acquired. Celebrate the improvement you've got were given made in transferring your mind-set and embracing a extra empowering narrative.

Exercise three: Affirmations for Positive Self-Image

Create a list of affirmations that replicate a super self-image and decorate your worthiness of affection, connection, and healthful relationships. These affirmations must be customized to resonate with you on a deep emotional diploma.

Write your affirmations within the gift disturbing, the use of effective and empowering language. For example, "I am deserving of real connection and love" or "I embody vulnerability as a electricity."

Repeat those affirmations every day, each aloud or silently, as a practice of self-affirmation and self-love. Allow those outstanding statements to permeate your subconscious mind, converting the antique awful beliefs with new, empowering truths.

Exercise 4: Creating a New Narrative

Now it's time to create a extremely-cutting-edge narrative for your self. Imagine the man or woman you aspire to be in relationships—a person who embodies solid attachment, vulnerability, and healthful connection. Write a quick tale or description of this best model of your self, the use of super language and sensory statistics.

Capture the essence of this new narrative via expressing the way you display up in relationships, the way you speak, and the manner you navigate traumatic conditions. Embrace the capabilities, beliefs, and behaviors that beneficial resource strong attachment and real connection.

After developing your new narrative, mirror at the emotions it conjures up within you. Visualize your self embodying this new version of your self, and receive as actual with to your capability to step into this transformed truth.

Remember, pricey soul, that rewriting restricting ideals is a powerful act of self-transformation. Embrace the technique of difficult horrible self-talk, cultivating wonderful affirmations, and developing a cutting-edge narrative that aligns with the consistent attachment you desire. Embody the abilities and ideals of the character you aspire to be, and have an excellent time every bounce forward on this adventure of boom and recuperation.

Developing Emotional Resilience

Exercise 1: Emotional Regulation Techniques

Emotional law is the important thing to developing resilience and navigating the u.S.And downs of relationships. Explore severa strategies that can help you regulate your feelings successfully.

Experiment with deep respiratory wearing events, grounding strategies, or mindfulness practices to carry your self into the winning second and discover inner calm.

Identify the techniques that resonate with you the most and make a list of those you find useful. Incorporate the ones techniques into your each day normal to cultivate emotional well-being and construct resilience within the face of difficult emotions.

Exercise 2: Self-Soothing Strategies

Developing self-soothing techniques can provide consolation and assist sooner or later of moments of emotional misery. Reflect on sports activities or practices that carry you a enjoy of comfort, peace, and solace. It can be taking note of soothing tune, wearing out slight physical motion like taking walks or yoga, or indulging in innovative shops collectively with writing or painting.

Create a self-soothing toolkit which include the strategies that resonate with you. Use this toolkit to show to whilst you want a second of respite or whilst emotions experience overwhelming. Explore those techniques with kindness and compassion, letting them nourish your emotional well-being.

Exercise 3: Expressing and Validating Emotions

Expressing and validating feelings is important for constructing emotional resilience. Take time to select out and honor your emotions without judgment.

Reflect on techniques to explicit your emotions constructively, at the facet of thru journaling, talking to a trusted friend or therapist, or accomplishing revolutionary retailers.

Practice self-compassion via acknowledging and validating your emotions. Remember that your feelings are valid and need to be heard and understood. Engage in self-mirrored image and discover the underlying dreams and desires at the back of your feelings.

Exercise four: Coping with Fear of Vulnerability

Fear of vulnerability can restriction emotional intimacy and connection. Take a brave breakthrough thru exploring strategies to deal with this fear. Begin through reflecting on the muse reasons of your worry and the tactics wherein it manifests in your relationships.

Challenge your worry of vulnerability thru step by step beginning up and sharing your mind, emotions, and desires with relied on people. Start with small steps and feature amusing every act of vulnerability, irrespective of how seemingly insignificant.

Practice self-compassion and remind your self that vulnerability is a strength, not a susceptible element. Embrace the discomfort that would rise up and understand that true connection and deep intimacy are born from vulnerability.

After attempting those bodily games, take a 2d to mirror in your enjoy. How did training emotional regulation strategies, exploring self-soothing techniques, expressing and validating emotions, and coping with fear of vulnerability impact your emotional resilience? Embrace the boom and improvement you've got were given made in this direction of recovery and resilience-constructing.

Chapter 15: Building Secure Relationships

Exercise 1: Recognizing Healthy Relationship Patterns

Take a 2d to reflect on the lovable tapestry of healthy courting patterns that foster consistent attachment.

Think approximately relationships on your life or in the lives of others that embody trends which embody trust, apprehend, assist, and open communication. Notice the moments of kindness, records, and real connection.

As you replicate, permit yourself to experience the warm temperature and love that emanate from those relationships. Capture the essence of these patterns to your coronary heart and thoughts. Embrace the perception that the ones healthful dating dynamics are not nice possible however additionally internal your benefit.

Exercise 2: Effective Communication Skills

Communication is the lifeblood of stable relationships. Explore and workout effective conversation talents that foster stable attachment. Engage in energetic listening, supplying your undivided interest and empathy. Speak your reality with honesty, kindness, and apprehend. Seek expertise and be open to particular views.

As you practice effective communication, be conscious the blossoming of connection and know-how that arises. Embrace the energy of terms and the healing they may be able to bring. Celebrate each 2d of real and heartfelt change as you nurture the bonds of regular attachment.

Exercise three: Establishing Boundaries

Boundaries are the guardians of healthy relationships. Reflect to your personal obstacles, those slight fences that honor and guard your desires, values, and emotions. Identify areas in which you can need to reinforce your limitations or create new ones.

As you set up and speak your obstacles, recognize the strength and self-respect it takes to honor your very own limits. Embrace the empowerment that comes from advocating for yourself and fostering an environment of mutual recognize on your relationships.

Exercise 4: Practicing Trust and Intimacy

Trust and intimacy are the pillars of stable attachment. Engage within the exercising of trust through way of starting your coronary heart and permitting others to appearance your actual self. Embrace vulnerability as a pathway to deep connection and emotional closeness.

As you practice obtain as actual with and intimacy, cherish the moments of shared vulnerability and emotional intimacy. Celebrate the bonds that develop stronger as you dare to open yourself up and invite others to do the identical. Remember that accept as true with is constructed through the years and nurtured through consistency, reliability, and compassionate records.

After trying the ones wearing activities, take a 2d to reflect on your revel in.

How did spotting wholesome courting patterns, practising effective conversation abilties, organising limitations, and working towards consider and intimacy effect your records of steady attachment and your capability to construct pleasing relationships? Celebrate your increase and decide to persevering with the adventure inside the path of solid and huge connections.

Chapter 16: Healing Inner Child Wounds

Exercise 1: Connecting with Your Inner Child

Take a second to connect to your internal toddler, that willing and harmless part of you that carries the accidents from the beyond. Imagine yourself as a infant on the same time as ultimate your eyes. Feel the emotions and sensations that arise internal you.

Extend a hand of love and compassion for your inner baby. Offer consolation, understanding, and reassurance. Let them comprehend which you are proper here for them now, that they may be regular, and that their voice topics.

After connecting at the aspect of your inner toddler, take a 2nd to magazine approximately the enjoy. Reflect on any feelings, memories, or insights that emerged. Embrace the preciousness of your inner little one and the recuperation adventure that lies earlier.

Exercise 2: Reparenting Your Inner Child

In this exercising, step into the position of a loving and nurturing decide for your internal little one. Visualize yourself because the compassionate guardian your greater younger self wished but might not have had. Imagine presenting them with the love, validation, and useful resource they deserved.

Write a letter on your inner infant, expressing your self-discipline to be their loving protector and manual. Share phrases of encouragement, understanding, and confirmation. Let them apprehend they will be deserving of affection and popularity.

After writing the letter, take a look at it aloud to yourself or your inner infant. Allow the terms to sink deep into your being, soothing the wounded elements indoors you. Embrace the electricity of reparenting and the transformative recuperation it could bring.

Exercise three: Healing Past Traumas

Healing beyond traumas is a courageous and transformative adventure. Take time to reflect at the traumas you've got got were given professional and their impact to your lifestyles. Honor the pain and emotions that get up as you delve into those sensitive areas.

Seek professional useful resource if had to manual you via the recuperation manner. Engage in trauma-informed practices such as remedy, EMDR, or somatic restoration modalities. Remember that restoration takes time and is a nonlinear method.

Practice self-compassion and self-care as you navigate the recuperation of beyond traumas. Prioritize your well-being and permit your self to method emotions in a secure and supportive environment. Embrace the resilience within you and the functionality to heal wounds which have affected your attachment style.

Exercise 4: Nurturing Your Inner Child

Engage in nurturing practices to guide your internal little one's recuperation. Identify sports activities that deliver delight, consolation, and a revel in of playfulness. It can be dancing, drawing, spending time in nature, or carrying out modern hobbies that ignite your imagination.

Integrate those nurturing sports into your every day life, making them a normal part of your ordinary. Embrace the inner toddler inside you and offer them the love, care, and attention they deserve. Nurture their curiosity, spontaneity, and experience of wonder.

After attempting the ones sporting sports, take a 2d to reflect on your experience. How did connecting collectively collectively along with your inner little one, reparenting, healing beyond traumas, and nurturing your inner little one effect your restoration journey?

Celebrate the courage and resilience you have verified, information that inner little one recovery is a transformative step within the path of consistent attachment and a greater interesting lifestyles.

Integrating Healing Practices

Exercise 1: Mindfulness and Self-Care Routines

Embrace the power of mindfulness and self-care as critical factors of your recovery journey. Set apart committed time each day to engage in mindfulness practices that promote self-interest and present-second interest. This might also embody meditation, deep breathing physical sports, or simply grounding yourself within the beauty of the present moment.

Incorporate self-care sporting events into your each day existence to nourish your mind, frame, and soul. Engage in sports that supply you delight, whether or no longer it's far taking a calming bath, going for a stroll in nature, analyzing a fave e book, or indulging in contemporary pursuits. Prioritize self-care as an act of self-love and a manner to refill your strength.

Exercise 2: Seeking Support from Trusted Individuals

Healing isn't always a solitary adventure. Reach out to trusted people who can provide assist, steering, and a listening ear. Share your stories, fears, and triumphs with folks who offer a secure and non-judgmental space as a way to specific your self authentically.

Identify the people on your existence who uplift and beneficial resource you. Surround yourself with a community of compassionate souls who can offer empathy, encouragement, and records. Lean on them whilst wanted, understanding that you are in no manner on my own on this direction of recovery and boom.

Exercise three: Applying Healing Strategies in Real-Life Situations

Take the restoration strategies you've got were given observed out and workout them in actual-life conditions. In hard moments or interactions, consciously supply focus in your attachment fashion, emotional triggers, and the equipment you have got got received. Pause, breathe, and pick out a reaction that aligns collectively together along with your restoration adventure.

Practice effective verbal exchange, emotional regulation, and vulnerability on the equal time as faced with courting demanding situations. Engage in self-reflected picture to apprehend your reactions and make conscious alternatives that promote stable attachment and real connection.

Exercise 4: Reflecting on Your Growth and Progress

www.ingramcontent.com/pod-product-compliance
Lightning Source LLC
Chambersburg PA
CBHW072157070526
44585CB00015B/1179